S A M P A I
KENPO

Michael Persons

EMPIRE BOOKS/AWP LLC
Los Angeles, CA.

Revised Edition First published in 2023 by AWP LLC/Empire Books.

EMPIRE BOOKS
P.O. Box 491788
Los Angeles, CA 90049

First Edition.

Library of Congress Catalog Number: ISBN-13: 978-1-949753-54-7

23 22 21 20 19 18 17 16 15 14 13 12

Library of Congress Cataloging-in-Publication Data

Sam Pai Kenpo / by Michael Persons. — 1st revised ed. p. cm. Includes index.

ISBN 978-1-949753-54-7 (pbk.: alk. paper)
1. Kenpo. 5. Martial arts--technique. 3. Large type books.
I. Title. GV1332.3.F715 20146069.815'3--dc24

2006012320.

PRINTED IN THE UNITED STATES OF AMERICA.

Dedication

Welcome to the Revised Edition of Sam Pai Kenpo. I dedicate this book to all the martial artists who have contributed to its rich 1,500-year history, as well as, present day and future martial artists. For a chronicle of the 1,500-year history of Kenpo go to: **www.7WindsKenpo.com.**

The written word allows us to pass on our legacy for future generations. When I wrote this book my goal was to preserve the art of Sam Pai Kenpo, which has morphed into 3 Shields Kenpo and now 7 Winds Kenpo. This has also continued in the writing of my two current martial arts adventure novels "The Warriors of Chilandra", which is the first book in the "Beyond Shazandras Series" and "The 7 Secret Scrolls". For information on my books, merchandise and Kenpo go to: **www.7WindsKenpo.com.**

The 2023 Revised Edition has the original 1982 version of Sam Pai Kenpo as well as added content and a 12-page interview from "Masters" Magazine.

Thank you for allowing me to share part of my 57-year journey from white belt to 10th Degree Black Belt, Grand Master of 7 Winds Kenpo.

Acknowledgements

I wish to acknowledge my respect to those people responsible for my life in Kenpo and those who helped me to write this book. To my father, who took me into our kitchen in Hawthorne, California one day, and taught me how to defend myself against a neighborhood bully. That bully was quite surprised the next time we encountered each other.

To Mr. Ed Parker, without whom, there would be no Kenpo in America today. He is truly a martial arts pioneer and master of this art. One has only to witness his demonstration of Kenpo to understand this.

To Mr. Joe Dimmick, who has been my teacher and friend since 1966. He is one of the finest martial artists I have known. He is creative, skillful, and as with Mr. Parker, his Kenpo skill is awe inspiring.

To Ed and Amanda Chambless whose friendship and support saw me through a very tough time in my life and encouraged me to author this book in 1982. Ed is my partner in the book and is an extremely skilled and accomplished martial artist. My thanks to Ed for writing my biography.

A special thanks to Jose M. Fraguas, who is dedicated to the preservation of martial arts history. He contacted me for an interview for *Masters Magazine* and in the process offered to publish this revised edition of Sam Pai Kenpo to assure that this art is not lost in time. His expertise, professionalism, and friendship are greatly appreciated.

About The Author

Michael Persons has been involved in the study of the martial arts since 1966; particularly, the study of Kenpo. When the first edition of Sam Pai Kenpo was released, the author had attained a fifth-degree black belt in the art. His training had been an arduous one spanning fifteen years.

The 2023 Revised Edition of Sam Pai Kenpo finds Michael Persons has continued to study to expand his knowledge and expertise in Kenpo and is now a 10th Degree Black Belt Grand Master. His current system has evolved and is now a martial arts system called 7 Winds Kenpo.

In keeping with the tradition of change and expansion of the system of Sam Pai Kenpo, Mr. Persons had made three major contributions by 1982: the first was the "Way of the Warrior" black belt form; the second was a quick moving, high energy, "Club Set"; and the third was "Tension Set". This third set is similar to the Sanchin Moving Meditation, combining continuous deep breathing and body tension in a dynamic exercise which develops the internal energy called "chi."

The author believes that with the power to destroy also comes the responsibility to heal. With this in mind, he turned his attention to the study and research of a number of internal healing arts. The study of herbs and their effect on human ailments has shown a high rate of success. Many modern-day medications are derived from herbal compounds. However, one must keep in mind to consult a medical doctor when these ailments persist as well as being mindful of allergies to any herbs that individuals might have.

He believes healthy eating habits, regular exercising and stretching contribute to all round health and improved focus to aid in the study of Kenpo and a better quality of life.

Michael Persons has also developed an herbal liniment which has shown itself to be effective to relieve the pain of sprains, bruises, strained muscles, headaches etc.

Table Of Contents

Foreword

This revised edition of Sam Pai Kenpo is being released for historical purposes. Our system has gone through many revisions since I began in February 1966. When I started, there were no names for the self-defense techniques. The instructor just had to call out a right punch or push, and the student at that level would respond with the appropriate technique.

When Grand Master Joe Dimmick formed his system in 1972, he changed four of the Parker forms: Short 1, Short 2, Long 1, and Long 3.

In my system, 7 Winds Kenpo, I kept all of the forms created by Grand Master Parker and Grand Master Dimmick plus added another 27 for a total of 51 forms. I wanted to honor both my teacher and his teacher as well.

In 1982, when this book was released, we did have names for our techniques but there were only seventeen techniques and four forms in what was the Orange Belt level. Short 1 Blocking Set is what I call Dimmick Short 1 today and Short Form 1 is now called Parker Short 1. So, you have two versions of Short 1. You also have the basic two-man staff set showing the right and left sides.

7 Winds Kenpo has changed since I created it in January 2002. Orange Belt level is the foundation or the bottom of the pyramid. There are 82 Basics, 5 Forms, consisting of Finger Set, Parker Short 1, Two Man Staff Set, Right and Left Sides, and Fighting Warrior Set 1. There are also 30 Self-Defense and Freestyle techniques in this level. Every level has a least one weapons form and one freestyle form through 1st Degree Black Belt. The self-defense and freestyle techniques ratio range from 4 in Orange Belt to as many as 12 in upper levels, the balance of the 30 being the self defense techniques.

This book served as a prototype for my training manuals which I make available to my students at every level. Dr. Ken Horup, who is working towards his 10th Degree Black Belt, and another student, Vince Mucci, is working towards his 7th Degree Black Belt; each has manuals up to their respective levels.

These manuals are in a 3-ring binder so if I make changes to the system, those pages can be easily replaced, and the manuals kept up-to-date.

I hope that in this manner there will always be a record of how it was done in 7 Winds Kenpo and anyone starting at the beginning could learn the terminology and follow through to the upper levels, provided that they have the training manuals. There are seventeen manuals altogether, ranging from Orange Belt to 10th Black.

I have always written down all of the material from my training sessions, coupled with notes given through the years I have compiled and organized what is now 7 Winds Kenpo. In the training manuals, I have explained every move we do in Kenpo: Blocks, punches, kicks, parries, breaks, takedowns, special weapons, forms, and self-defense techniques. Every move has a description of how to do it.

Beyond this historical book, I hope that it will inspire you to seek out a qualified Kenpo instructor and start your journey if you have not already begun. Mine has taken me 57 years thus far, and I feel like I have many more years to come. It has been a privilege to share my art with many wonderful people. Won't you join me on the path?

For more information on 7 Winds Kenpo and a chronicle of 1,500 years of Kenpo History, please visit my website at **www.7windskenpo.com.**

Kenpo History

Kenpo history can be traced back to a period around the 1600's and to the Shaolin Temple and their lineage of past and present masters. Beyond this, there are Kenpo techniques which go back into ancient history according to my research and my personal beliefs.

Kenpo (or Kempo) is a Japanese term which means "the way or law of the fist." Originating in China, this art made its way to Japan shortly before the 1600's and eventually came to Hawaii in 1936.

Daruma or Bodhidharma in Sanskrit was an Indian priest who promised his master that he would spread and develop the Zen Sect of Buddhism. He set out walking through India and China, eventually ending up at the Shaolin Temple. Upon arriving there, he discovered the weakened physical condition of the monks, Daruma taught them a series of exercises called the Eighteen Lohan to strengthen their bodies and enable them to better practice to strict meditation which was a part of this "new" religion.

Kenpo migrated to Japan around the 1600's and developed drastically within the following three hundred years. Virtually all of the circular movements taught at the Shaolin Temple were eliminated and only the linear (straight line) movements were retained. Kenpo had changed so much that the name was changed to Kosho-ryu Kenpo or "Old Pine Tree Style" Kenpo.

Kenpo migrated to Hawaii in 1936 under this name and was exposed to the public for the first time in 1942 at the Official Self-Defense Club at the Britania Mission in Honolulu.

William K. S. Chow began studying with the Kosho-ryu family and received a black belt from the current master, Mr. James Mitose. Chow had previously studied boxing and judo and had his share of street fighting experiences. He had also studied the Chinese martial arts which had been in his own family for generations. In these particular arts, he learned the circular movements which had been deleted from the Kosho-ryu. Chow then combined the circular movements of his family art and the linear movements of Kosho-ryu to develop his own form called Kenpo Karate. He opened a school and attracted many non-Asian students. Classes were very hard and extremely physical.

Ed Parker, a Hawaiian of royal ancestry, was directed to Chow by his first instructor, Frank Chow. He had to have a special introduction before he was admitted into the school. Parker had previously studied boxing and judo for four years. He earned his black belt from Chow in 1948. Chow instilled and encouraged the need for flexibility in the system. Parker decided to teach Kenpo as a profession and wanted Chow to come to the mainland with him to open a school. Parker went to Brigham Young University and returned to Hawaii in 1951 to join the Coast Guard during the Korean Conflict. Parker tried a second time after his duty with the Coast Guard but all of his plans fell through. When Parker finished college, he tried another time to get Chow to come to the United States but this did not seem to work out either. Chow gave Parker his very good blessings and told him that he was on his own.

Parker taught in the local police departments and at college during his days at the university. Bert Goodrich, brother-in-law to Vic Tanny, invited Parker to come to California and open up several gyms and introduce karate. By the time Parker arrived in California, American Health Studios had bought out the defunct Vic Tanny's gyms and with it went his plans for the future. Parker borrowed $300.00 from a friend and opened his own school by himself in 1956.

In that same year, Joe Dimmick began his training as a student under Parker and received his black belt in 1961. In 1965, Dimmick also received his black belt in a kung-fu style which combined the Hung-Gar and Choy Li Fut systems. Later, he received his black belt in the Chito-Ryu Style of Japanese karate. In 1965, in association with Parker, Dimmick opened his own school in Downey, California.

My own training began in 1966 with Dimmick. In 1972, I received my black belt under a rigid examination with Parker and Dimmick. In that same year, Dimmick founded his own system which is now known as Sam Pai Kenpo (Three Shields Kenpo) under the California Sam Pai Kenpo Association.

Sam Pai refers to the "Three Shields" which is the basis for this fighting defense system. This system is a combination of the three schools of martial arts which Dimmick has mastered. Kenpo is the foundation. Adding to the vast amount of techniques, Dimmick created and added advanced Kenpo forms such as "Flowing Palms," "Returning Shadow Set," "Creed Form," "Twin Dragon Set," "Two Man Staff Set," and a "Double Club Set." Dimmick also revised the intermediate Kenpo forms called the "Short One," "Short Two," "Long One" and "Long Three." He also added a "Two Man Staff Set" to his repetoire. In 1978, Dimmick was awarded an eighth degree black belt by the Sam Pai Kenpo Black Belt Committee. He has truly followed in the footsteps of his instructor, Ed Parker and developed his "vocabulary" by making more "words, sentences and paragraphs" from his alphabet of information obtained through sixteen years of instruction from Parker.

In 1980, Andre Ouellette and myself received our fifth degree black belt and are the first to have the honor and distinction of being Dimmick's highest ranking black belts. Andre Ouellette operates a commercial school in Fountain Valley, California, Most Sam Pai Kenpo instructors, however, teach privately out of their homes.

Definition Of Sam Pai Kenpo

The principle of kenpo is economy of motion. The basis for our defense, the Three Shields or Sam Pai, is our basic blocking defense and the most practical and sensible kenpo method in use today.

With the application of the Three Shields principle of defense, we assume a neutral bow position or fighting stance immediately. This cuts the target from a full width of the body to one half or a side target. We further divide the target in half by employing a center-line defense. We block off of this center-line, thus never defending more than a quarter of the body width at any one time. With this method you do not have to have the reactions of a black belt, only a working knowledge of the Three Shields principle. With the knowledge of the Three Shields principle, you can handle the average situation. As your skill and reactions grow, so will your ability to defend yourself. While the system does have techniques which are for committed attacks, the beginner does not have to rely on these to defend himself. Your opponent won't let you try your technique over and over again until you get it right. Therefore, by simply learning the Three Shields principles, the beginner, whose reactions will be mechanical in nature, is able to efficiently defend himself.

As you proceed through the instructional portion of the book, I would like you to feel that I am speaking directly to you and that you are in an actual class.

Class Etiquette

Entering the work out area, the student shows respect by performing a short bow. This is done by placing the left foot slightly forward with all of your weight resting on the rear, right foot. The hands are: right hand in a fist with the left open palm over the first knuckle of the right hand at about collar bone level. Return to a normal standing position and enter the work-out area. Respect is also paid in the same manner when leaving the work-out area.

Classes, whether private or group, begin with the students in rows facing the instructor. Lined up and standing with their feet together, the command "position" is given. This signals the students to step out with their left foot to a square horse stance with the hands in the same position as the short bow.

At this point a second command, "creed" is given, the students now repeat the Sam Pai Kenpo Creed:

"I come to you with only Sam Pai Kenpo, my empty hands.

I have no weapons, but should I be forced to defend myself, my principles, or my honor, should it be a matter of life or death, right or wrong, then here are my weapons, Sam Pai Kenpo, my empty hands."

The third command "up" is given, signaling the students to step back up with the left foot as the hands circle overhead. At the highest position overhead, the hands are like tiger claws and continue down to each side as if clawing an opponent on each side of you. (1) Remaining in this position, the students go right into "salutation:" (2) The right foot turns out and steps forward slightly preparing to accept all of the body weight. As the foot moves the right fist cocks to the right shoulder with the left hand covering it in an open palm manner. The left foot steps forward with the ball of the foot touching. As the foot plants down, the hands move down in front to collar bone height with the right fist covered on the first knuckle with the open palm of the left hand. Only five percent of the body weight is on the front left foot and ninety-five percent is on the right rear foot. The left foot steps straight back slightly behind the right foot as the student turns his hands, back to back. Circling them down towards the body, the student comes back out turning the palms up as the hands are pulled to the hips. The right foot steps back to the left at the same time. The hands come up in front forming the Three Shields symbol. First, the left hand is in the lead. The student shifts to the right hand in the lead. He brushes the left hand by the left thigh and the right hand brushes the right thigh. Then do a double palm push down. We have a joke in our school that, if you can master the salutation and handshake, the rest of the system is easy.

The command, "down for meditation" is given and the students sit down in place, crossed legged with the hands clasped and the index fingers extended with the finger tips touching. The back is straight. The eyes are closed and the student begins breathing deeply. Breathe in through the nose and out through the mouth (which is kept open slightly). The tongue rests on the roof of the mouth. The breathing need not be audible but should be relaxed. The students should try to concentrate on the finger tips and try to feel his own pulse beat.

Meditation is done at the beginning of each class to clear the mind of all that has gone on that day. "Try to make your mind receptive to what you are about to learn and forget for the next couple of hours, your problems." I usually say something like this at the beginning of the class and then let them sit quietly for a few minutes. Then I have a "saying of the day" which I repeat to them and give them a few more minutes to think of its meaning. This will put them in the proper frame of mind to begin the actual class. I will not go into the basic warm-up exercises at this time. However, it is most important that the students warm-up to avoid strained or pulled muscles.

Breathing Techniques

We do three types of breathing exercises. All three are performed in the following manner. On the inhale, extend your stomach out and on the exhale, retract the stomach back in. This is the type of breathing we do naturally as children but, somewhere along the line, we began breathing from our chest, reversing the process and making our breathing shallow and short as opposed to the deep breathing of our childhood. Could this be why children seem to have endless energy? Many Orientals believe it to be so. Breathing in this manner not only increases energy but also longevity.

We use this technique in three different ways. The first is called fast and is performed by inhaling and exhaling quickly. This is usually done after strenuous exercise to catch your breath. We usually perform two fast breaths before going on to the next one.

The second method is performed by inhaling fast and exhaling with a little tension. Your inhale in the same manner but tense the stomach area as you exhale. This is called fast-tension breathing.

The third method is called fast-slow tension breathing and is performed by inhaling fast, as in the previous two techniques, but the exhale is done slowly. Try to force all of the air from the abdomen-stomach area.

This is the only abdomen work that we do in our system and it is sufficient to condition the stomach when done regularly.

The Clock Method

Standing in the center of a clock formation, it is easy to move in any direction by simply calling out the number and moving your foot to that number. Step your right foot back to 6:00 or forward to 12:00, you have an immediate picture in your mind of where you are moving. Some systems use north, south, east and west but you cannot always be sure of your directions when you are in an unfamiliar room. The clock method gives you a clear mental picture, 12:00 is always in front of you. You can also move the clock off of the floor and place it in front of you mentally so that if you were to strike down you could be striking to 6:00. A chop could be delivered at a 1:00–2:00 angle to the neck. This gives a very clear picture and can be easily visualized.

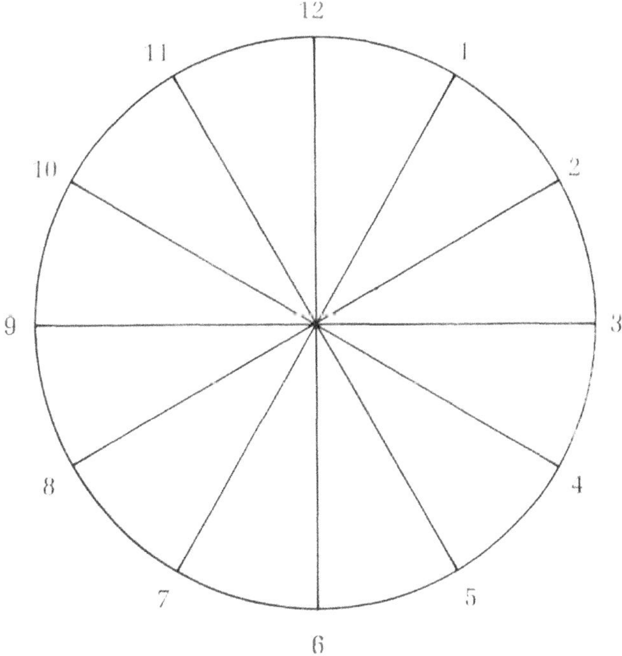

STANCES

Stances or horse training in many traditional schools last for as much as two years. This is the foundation of the martial arts and many teachers do not show other techniques until the stances are mastered. This method also served to weed out the insincere students. There are over twenty stances in the system of which you will be learning the first six. Remember, this is your foundation so it must be strong. A house on a weak foundation will tumble down when confronted by the first adverse wind. Do not overlook this important part of your training. The differences will show up immediately.

Set Salutation

Salutation is either used as a formal greeting or a signal that you are ready to perform a set. You have already seen the short version as well as our regular salutation. This is the set salutation.

(1) From a standing position,

(2) the right foot turns out and steps forward slightly, preparing to accept all of your body weight. As the foot moves, the left arm cocks across the chest to the right shoulder, palm open and facing forward. The right fist rises in front of the open palm to designate the form or set number. For short form one, make a fist and extend your first or index finger up but in a bent position, half finger. If it were long form one, you would extend your finger straight up in front of the open palm.

(3) Close the right hand back to a fist immediately so that only those who know what to look for will know what form you are doing.

(4) As the left foot plants forward, the hands move down in front, collar bone height, with the right fist covered on the first knuckle by the left open plam. Only five percent of your weight is on the front left foot while ninety-five percent is on the rear right foot.

(5) Turn your hands back to back.

(6) The left foot steps straight back slightly behind your right. Circle them down towards your body.

(7) As you come back out, turn the palms up

(8) and as you pull your hands to your hips, step the right foot back to the left at the same time.

(9) Step the left foot out to 9:00 to a square horse, circle your hands overhead and form a triangle, I call "temple."

(10) One hand distance lower form "fist" done by closing the right hand to make a fist and cover it with the left palm.

(11) One hand distance lower form "prayer."

(12) One hand distance lower form "fist" again at collar bone height.

Step back "up" with your left foot, circle your hands overhead. At the highest position the hands are like tiger claws and continue down to each side.

Standing position.

The right foot turns out and steps forward slightly preparing to accept all of the body's weight. Simultaneously, the left arm cocks across the chest to the right shoulder with the palm open and facing forward. The right fist rises in front of the open palm to designate the form or set number.

Close the right hand into a fist immediately.

As the left foot plants forward, the hands move down in front to about the height of the collar bone. The right fist is covered on the first knuckle by the left open palm.

Turn your hands so they are back to back.

The left foot steps back slightly to a point behind your right foot. Circle your hands down towards the body.

As you come back out, turn the palms upwards.

As you pull your hands to your hips, the right foot steps back to the left.

Step the left foot out to 9:00 into a square horse position. Circle your hands overhead and form a triangle with the fingers called a "temple."

At a distance of one hand, lower the form "fist" which is done by closing the right hand to make a fist and cover it the left palm.

At one hand distance, lower into the form, "prayer."

At one hand distance, lower into form "fist" which is now at collar bone height again.

Square Horse

(1) Start with your feet together and hands at your sides.

(2) Step your left foot out to 9:00, your feet are parallel to each other, knees are bent and slightly out as if you are on the back of a horse. Your hands are cocked to your hips. The weight distribution is fifty-fifty.

Start with your feet together and your hands at your sides.

The left foot steps out to 9:00 with your feet parallel to each other and your knees slightly bent. This stance resembles riding a horse. Your hands are cocked to your hips. The weight distribution of the legs and feet is fifty-fifty.

Four Square Foot Pattern

(1) In a square horse, step the right foot to the left foot, turn to the left and step the right foot out to 12:00, now you are facing 9:00.

(2) Step the left foot to the right foot, turn to the left and step the left foot out to 3:00, now you are facing 6:00.

(3) Step the right foot to the left foot, turn to the left and step the right foot out to 6:00, now you are facing 3:00.

(4) Step the left foot to the right, turn again to the left and step out to 9:00 with the left foot, once again facing 12:00, the beginning position. This is the left side because your first move was toward the left. Now repeat the process for the right side starting with the left foot stepping and turn to the right.

Start in a square horse facing 12:00.

Your right foot steps to the left foot.

Turn to the left and the right foot steps out to 12:00. You are now facing 9:00.

Now, the left foot steps to the right foot.

Turn to the left and the left foot steps out to 3:00. You are now facing 6:00.

The right foot steps to the left foot.

Turn to the left and the right foot steps out to 6:00. You are now facing 3:00.

The left foot steps to the right foot.

Turn again to the left and step out to 9:00 with the left foot. You are now facing the original direction at 12:00.

Neutral Bow

This is the basic fighting stance. (1) From a standing position (2) step the right foot back to 6:00. You should now be in a square horse facing off at about 2:00. Turn your upper part of the body slightly forward so that your lead shoulder is pointing toward 12:00. Your feet should be parallel and in a front toe, back heel alignment. Think about standing over a staff on the floor which is laying on a 12:00 6:00 line. Now place the left toe on the left side of the staff at 12:00 and the right heel on the right side of the staff at 6:00. The hand position is, left hand in a fist down the center of the body with the fist at about chin level. The right arm is across the body at waist level, also in a closed fist position. This is the Three Shields fighting position. The weight distribution is fifty-fifty.

From a standing position.

The right foot steps back to 6:00. Your feet are parallel to each other with the toes and heels aligned with each other respectively.

Four Square Foot Pattern

(1) In a square horse, step the right foot to the left foot, turn to the left and step the right foot out to 12:00, now you are facing 12:00 with the hands in Three Shields.

(2) Second, step the left foot to the right foot, turn to the left and step the left foot out to 3:00, now you are facing 3:00 with the hands in Three Shields.

(3) Third, step the right foot to the left foot, turn to the left and step the right foot out to 6:00, now you are facing 6:00 with the hands in Three Shields.

(4) Fourth, step the left foot to the right, turn again to the left and step out to 9:00 with the left foot, now you are facing 9:00 with the hands in Three Shields. This is the left side because your first move was toward the left. Now repeat the process for the right side starting with the left foot stepping and turn to the right.

For a variation, as you step into position, face the opposite direction. For example, when you step the right foot to the left and step out to 12:00, turn and face back to 6:00.

Assume a square horse.

The right foot steps to the left foot and then turn yourself to the left stepping the right foot out to 12:00. You are now facing 12:00 with the hands in a Three Shields position.

The left foot steps to the right foot.

Turn to the left and step the left foot out to 3:00. You are now facing 3:00 with the hands still in the Three Shields position.

The left foot steps to the right foot.

Turn to the left and step the right foot out to 6:00 with the hands in the Three Shields position. You are now facing 6:00.

Step the left foot out to the right.

Turn again to the left and step out to 9:00 with the left foot. You are now facing 9:00 with the hands still in the Three Shields position.

Finish the movement by moving the hands back the square horse position.

Checking Neutral Bow-Angle

This means that you continue to move so that your center-line is not open to attack. You close yourself off to a groin attack by closing your stance. This is the proper alignment to protect yourself against a groin attack.

Continue to line up your body so your center-line is not open to attack. This is the proper alignment to protect yourself against a groin attack.

Checking Neutral Bow-Contact

During a technique or close-in fighting you can actually make contact with your lower leg to your opponent's leg thus checking the leg from kicking or scooping you. This is an example of contact being made on your opponent's leg.

Example of contact being made to your opponent's leg.

Forward Bow

Move the right foot back to 6:00, neutral bow.

Shift the hips forward by straightening the right leg and shifting the heel out. Shift your weight forward by bending your front, left leg. Moving from a fifty-fifty weight distribution to sixty-forty, with the sixty percent on your front bent leg. Your hands should be in a Three Shields formation.

This stance is used to gain distance and add power while punching without going off balance. The shifting of the hips while delivering the punch generates the power. This stance is used for fighting uphill, such as on the stairs while maintaining a strong stance.

The right foot is back to 6:00 in the neutral bow position.

Shift the hips forward by straightening the
right leg out and shifting the heel outwards.
Shift your weight forward by bending your
front, left leg. Your weight distribution is
transferred from a fifty-fifty to a sixty-forty
shift. Keep your hands in the Three Shields
position.

Finish the movement by shifting back to the
neutral bow.

Reverse Bow

(1) Move the right foot back to 6:00, neutral bow.

(2) Shift the hips to the rear by straightening the front, left leg and shifting the heel forward towards the opponent. Bend the rear leg, shifting your weight from a fifty-fifty weight distribution to a sixty-forty with sixty percent on the rear bent leg. As you shift back, your hands shift from Three Shields to left palm push down and right parry in front of your face at about chin level.

This stance gives you distance from your opponent in a close position. You can also strike with the front hand using the shift for cross-pull striking power. See Whipping Chop in the Special Weapons section. You can also use this for fighting downhill, such as on stairs while maintaining a strong stance.

The right foot is back to 6:00 in a neutral bow stance.

Shift the hips to the rear by straightening
the front left leg and shifting the heel forward towards the opponent. Bend the rear
leg, shifting your weight from a fifty-fifty
weight distribution to sixty-forty with emphasis on the rear bent leg. Your front hand
drops to a palm push down position and the
rear hand parries the front of the face with
the elbow kept close to the chest.

Finish by shifting back to the neutral bow
position.

One Leg Or Golden Chicken

(1) To practice this stance, begin by stepping the left foot out to 9:00 and cock the hands to your hips.

(2) Take a short step with the right foot to adjust your weight as the left foot comes off the ground. Cock the foot close to the right leg without touching it. The foot should be parallel to the ground, ready to deliver a knife edge kick. The knee should be pointing off at about 10:00. Your hands should be in the Three Shields position with your lead hand corresponding to the same leg which is off the ground.

This stance is used to avoid a foot sweep or to side step a frontal attack. The hand position can vary with the student and the nature of the situation.

Start in a square horse.

Take a short step with the right foot adjusting your weight as the left foot comes off the ground. Cock the foot close to the right leg but without touching it.

Finish the movement by planting back down to the originial square horse position.

FOOT MOVEMENTS

Foot Movements are the systematic methods we use to move forward, backwards or change directions. As you develop the quickness and discrimination, foot movements will keep you just out of your opponent's reach or will close the gap with your opponent at the proper moment of attack.

Moving Neutral Bow

This is the basic movement for going forward or reverse. It amounts to walking forward or backwards kenpo style.

(1) Assume a Neutral Bow stance with the right leg back to 6:00, your hands are in a Three Shields formation.

(2) To move forward turn the left foot forward slightly as you step the right foot forward arching by the left foot in a half moon movement.

(3) At the center-point the feet are close together and the groin is protected.

(4) Finish the move by planting the right foot forward in a neutral bow and shift the left heel into position. The hands shift with the feet so that you start with the left hand forward and at the center-point the hands go through a parry and the right hand moves to the forward position. Even in this vulnerable forward movement, we have checked the groin area from attack and the hands are parrying, always checking, protecting your upper body and head.

(5) To move backwards, shift the left heel back as

(6) the right foot moves backwards arching the left foot in the same manner as moving forward. As the right foot plants back, shift the left foot into position. Hands move in the same manner, pull the right hand back, and shift the left foot into position. Hands move in the same manner, pull the right hand back, shift your left hand forward as the step is made.

This movement is used primarily as an adjustment or safe way to change positions. Never change positions by moving forward into an opponent.

Begin in a neutral bow with the right leg back to 6:00.

Move forward by turning the left foot forward slightly as you step the right foot forward. The left foot arches in a half-moon movement. The feet should be relatively close together and the groin is well protected.

Finish by planting the right forward in a neutral bow stance.

To move backwards, shift the left heel back.

The right foot moves backwards also arching the foot in the same half-moon movement.

Finish by planting the right foot back in a neutral bow stance.

Step And Drag Shuffle

(1) Assume a neutral bow position, right foot back to 6:00, hands are in Three Shields position. This movement is one of the quickest ways of moving forward and backwards to either attack or retreat.

(2) Depending upon the penetration desired, take a six inch step forward with the front foot.

(3) The back foot drags up the same six inches to maintain a good fighting stance. You should end up in the same neutral bow you started in. Remember, both feet should move the same distance to avoid overextending yourself and ending up in an awkward position.

(4) To move backwards, step back with the rear foot the desired distance and

(5) drag back with the front foot the same distance ending in a good neutral bow stance.

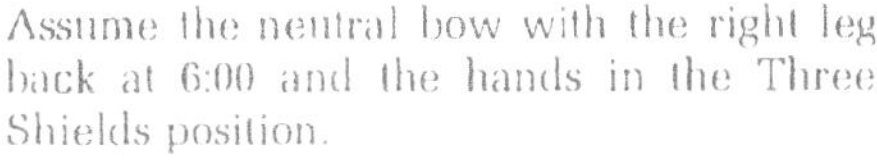

Assume the neutral bow with the right leg back at 6:00 and the hands in the Three Shields position.

Take a six inch step forward with the front foot.

The back foot drags up six inches to maintain a good fighting stance.

From the neutral bow, move backwards.

Step back with the rear foot.

Drag back the front foot the same direction.

Crossout Retreat

This movement is used to get away from an opponent either at the finish of a self-defense technique or in a fight situation when you need room to think or run.

(1) Work out of a neutral bow, right foot back to 6:00, hands are in Three Shields.

(2) The left foot crosses over the right and plants at about 5:00. Continue to keep your eye on the opponent.

(3) Step the right foot back to 5:00. You should end up in a neutral bow only about three feet away from the opponent.

Neutral bow with the right leg back to 6:00
and the hands in a Three Shields position.

The left foot steps over the top of the right, planting to about a 5:00 into a twisted position.

Step the right foot back to 5:00 back to a neutral bow position finishing the movement.

Attack Pattern

This is our foot pattern for attacking during an offensive thrust forward.

(1) Assume a neutral bow, right foot back to 6:00, hands are in Three Shields. After setting your opponent up with fakes, or before they get set up would be the best time to use this tactic.

(2) The front foot takes a step forward, much the same as the "step and drag shuffle."

The lead hand remains in position or could be used as a lunge strike at this point.

(3) Cross forward with the rear leg planting between 12:00 1:00.

(4) The final move is to step forward with the left leg, finishing in a neutral bow.

We strike on the first step making this a very quick and effective technique. The extra step in the beginning gives you the extra quickness and greater distancing for the attack.

Assume a neutral bow with the right leg
back to 6:00 and the hands in Three Shields.

Take a step forward to 12:00 with the front foot in the same manner as in the step and drag shuffle.

Step with the right foot forward to a cross position at about 1:00.

Step the left foot forward to 12:00 into a neutral bow.

Cover

This movement is done to change directions and still maintain a good stance.

(1) Assume a neutral bow, right leg back to 6:00, hands are in Three Shields. In this front toe-back heel position you will notice that the lead foot will be between 11:00 12:00.

(2) Move the front foot in toward the back foot, in a "V" pattern and

(3) step back out to a 12:00 1:00 position as you turn and face 6:00. The "V" step is only a slight adjustment in and out as you turn and not a deep movement where you will be stepping to your back foot.

We always move the foot farthest away from any opponent. When you finish with the opponent at 12:00 and another approaches from 6:00, your lead foot moves. In this way if you are pushed in the middle of the move before you can turn around, you will fall back into a neutral bow. If you were to move the foot closest to the oncoming opponent and be pushed in the middle of the movement it would throw you off balance.

Start in a neutral bow.

Move the front left foot in towards the back foot in a "V" pattern.

Step back out to a 12:00 to 1:00 position as you turn and face towards 6:00 assuming a neutral bow position.

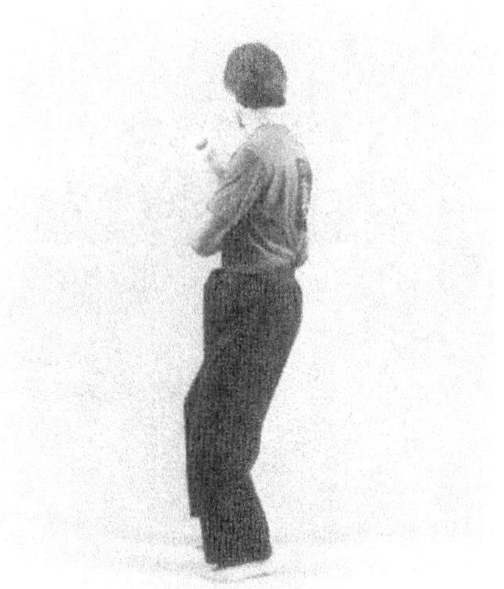

To cover back, the right foot steps in towards the back foot in the same "V" pattern.

Step back out to a 5:00 or 6:00 position as you turn and face 12:00 assuming a neutral bow position.

Cover-Correct Method

When the opponent approaches from the rear.

Move the foot farthest away from him.

In this way, if you are in the middle of your movement before you have the opportunity to turn around, you will naturally fall back into a neutral bow.

Cover-Incorrect Method

When the opponent approaches you from behind.

You move the closest foot towards him. He can push you and attack.

This will throw you off balance.

BLOCKS—THREE SHIELDS

Blocks are the basic method of defense and the essence of the Three Shields of Sam Pai Kenpo. This revolutionary method of defense will teach the novice to defend himself efficiently in a minimal amount of time. Once this skill is perfected, his defense will be virtually invulnerable. Being the most important technqiue he will learn the student must practice it faithfully.

In Three Shields, all blocks are done from a neutral bow. At first, remain stationary. After you feel comfortable with the blocks, use a step and drag shuffle moving backwards. You execute the block on the step portion of the shuffle movement.

The old method of accepting an attack straight on and having to react like a black belt to a situation has been all but eliminated. Wondering what the attack will be will no longer cause anymore tension in an already hostile situation. This method uses a center-line position, somewhat like Wing Chun kung-fu. However, unlike Wing Chun, we apply this in a neutral bow position, immediately cutting our target down from full body width to a half body width. In addition, by applying the center-line concept, we are defending only a quarter of our body width at any one time. There are circumstances where you may have a double punch coming in at the same time but this can be handled easily with distance. Simply shuffle back out of reach. Thus, after a basic understanding of the Three Shields concepts you will be able to defend against the attacker.

Inward

(1) From the center-line position,
(2) turn the wrist inward, strike to the outside of your body and
(3) return immediately back to the center-line.

This block is applied to an attack which comes to the inside of your body. Never go beyond the limits of the body as the retraction to the center-line will also turn into an over-reaction. And if a second punch is coming, it emphasizes this over-reaction.

Assume a neutral bow with the left leg back to 6:00 and the hands in a Three Shields center-line position.

Turn the wrist inward and strike to the outside of your body.

Return immediately back to the center-line.

Never go beyond the limits of the body as
the retraction back to the center-line can
easily become an over-reaction.

Outward

(1) From the center-line position,

(2) strike outward with the back side of your arm to the outside of your body and

(3) return immediately back to the center-line. This block is applied for an attack to the outside of the body.

(2a) Never go beyond the limits of the body.

Neutral bow with the left leg back to 6:00 and the hands in a Three Shields center-line position.

Strike outwards with the back side of your
arm to the outside of your body.

Return immediately back to the center-line
position.

Again, never go beyond the limits of your
body.

Elbow

(1) From the center-line position,

(2) drop your elbow to your hip and

(3) return immediately back to your center-line. This block is usually for a reverse or upper-cut punch or could be for front kick to ribs.

(2a) On this block, the biggest mistake is made by bending the body forward when dropping the elbow to the hip; you expose your face and are dangerously off balance.

Assume a neutral bow with the left leg back to 6:00 and the hands in a Three Shields center-line position.

Drop your elbow to your hip.

Return immediately back to the center-line position.

In this block, the biggest error is bending the body forward when dropping the elbow from the hip. Always maintain good posture.

Downward

(1) From the center-line position,

(2) Drop your back fist across the groin to the outside of your leg and

(3) return immediately back to your center-line. This block is usually for a front or roundhouse kick to the groin or body.

(2a) The problem here arises, once again by going beyond the limits of the body. The reaction time is cut down by initially over-reacting thus making you vulnerable.

Assume a neutral bow with the left leg back to 6:00 and the hands in a Three Shields center-line position.

Drop your back fist across the groin to the outside of your leg.

Return immediately back to the center-line position.

Here, another potential problem arises. By going beyond the limits of the body and over-reacting, you cut down your reaction time and expose yourself to attack.

Touch

(1) From the center-line position,

(2) take a short step back to 6:00 with the rear leg, draw your front leg up to a one leg stance, the rear hand drops to "downward" position and the front hand drops to "elbow" touching about 3–4 inches back from the end of your knee.

(3) Plant your front foot down next to your back foot and

(4) step back to 6:00, with the back foot to a neutral bow.

The mistake is made when the knee does not line up with the hip thus exposing the groin.

The first three blocks are where the term "Three Shields" originates, however, there are more than twenty blocks that are a part of the Three Shields system.

Assume a neutral bow with the left leg back to 6:00 and the hands in a Three Shield center-line position.

Take a short step back to 6:00 with the rear left leg. Assume a one-legged stance by drawing your front right foot up. The rear hand drops to a "downward" position and the front hand drops to a "elbow" touching position about three to four inches back from the knee.

Plant your front foot down next to your back foot.

Step back to 6:00 with the back foot into a neutral bow position.

One must line the knee up with the hip or the groin is left exposed.

Block Of Disturbance: Hip

This type of block disturbs the normal motion of the opponent either before they can launch an attack or at the end of a self-defense technique as a finishing movement.

(1) This block to the hip can be done at anytime you find yourself in a position of planting forward into the opponent where you have doubled him over and the hip is exposed.

(2) As you plant forward, extend your arm to a straight palm or like the old "straight arm" technique used in football, striking the hip. Use your body weight while planting forward to finish your technique and knock the opponent to the floor. See Evading the Storm in the self-defense technique section of this book for an application.

This block to the hip is done anytime you find yourself in a position of planting forward into the opponent when he is exposed and vulnerable.

As you plant forward, extend your arm into a straight palm to strike the hip. Use your body weight in planting forward to finish the technique.

PARRIES

Parries are methods of redirecting your opponents oncoming force with the open hand. These are a tremendous asset to the Three Shields method of blocking and give the student all he will need to ward-off any attack.

Inward

(1) Practice this move in a square horse.

(2) For a left hand attack, either punch or push, your right open palm comes up to the center-line and intercepts the opponent's hand.

(3) Direct it to the outside of the body making your hand follow an imaginary line as if going down the side of a triangle. This redirects the oncoming force to the outside of your body rather than meeting force with force.

Start in a square horse position.

Your right open palm comes up to the center-line and intercepts the opponent's hand.

Direct the hand to the outside of the body.

Variation

(1) In a square horse,

(2) bring your open palm up to your shoulder and

(3) deflect the oncoming hand on a forty-five degree angle with the heel palm.

Start in a square horse.

Bring your open palm up to your shoulder.

Deflect the oncoming hand at a forty-five degree angle with the heel palm.

Inward/Outward Palm Up

(1) Start in a square horse position.

(2) As a left push comes towards you, step the right foot forward to 12:00 and execute a right inward parry.

(3) Your left hand comes straight up on the outside of your right hand as if you were going to brush your hair back, outward parry.

(4) Drop your arm down in a vertical position by lowering your elbow. The wrist is bent back and checks the opponent's arm.

Start in a square horse position.

Step with the right foot forward to 12:00 and execute a right inward parry.

Your left hand comes straight up on the outside of your right hand as if you are going to brush your hair back. This is the outward parry.

Drop your arm down in a vertical position by lowering your elbow. The wrist is bent back and checks the opponent's arm.

Extended Outward

(1) Practice this move in a square horse.

(2) For a right hand attack, either push or punch or an overhead attack, the open right hand travels across your body to your left shoulder, facing the palm towards yourself.

(3) Turn your palm facing out and extend it to the outside of your body.

NOTE: This is for practice only. We always use an inward parry prior to the extended outward parry to give a measure of safety. Always remember, we never leave ourselves open. When one hand is extended, the other is retracted, checking close to the body. See Evading the Storm for an example of this combination in the self-defense technique section.

Start in a square horse position.

The open right hand travels across your
body to your left shoulder with the palm
facing towards yourself.

Turn your palm facing out and extend it to
the outside of your body.

KICKS

These seven kicks give you a method of attack using the ball, top, side and heel of your foot as well as your knee to strike your opponent from long or close ranges. Kick with power but perfect the technique because it will be quickness and skill that penetrates your opponent's defense.

Front Snap

(1) Assume a neutral bow with your right leg back to 6:00, hands are in Three Shields.

(2) Pivot the front left foot slightly forward, while bringing the right knee up and pointing at the desired target.

(3) As the knee reaches its high point, extend the leg out striking with the ball of the foot to the target.

(4) Retract the leg even faster than it struck out. This causes a vacuum and creates a bull whip effect or explosion of power at the end of the snap(s). Plant the foot back into a neutral bow and pivot your front foot back into position.

For a closer kick, use the top of the foot striking, usually, to the groin or the face (if your opponent is bent over).

Assume the neutral bow with the right leg back to 6:00 and the hands in a Three Shields position.

Pivot the front left foot slightly forward while bringing the right knee up and pointing it at the target.

As the knee reaches its high point, extend the leg out striking the target with the ball of the foot.

Retract the leg faster than the initial strike.

Plant the foot back into a neutral bow position.

Back Snap

(1) To practice this technique assume a standing position and imagine your opponent positioned behind you.

(2) Cock the foot up in front by raising the knee,

(3) bend forward slightly and extend the leg back, striking with the heel of your foot and then

(4) retract the foot back and plant the foot down. As you become more skillful in this technique you will be able to kick right from the floor eliminating two steps, not cocking the leg up. Whichever leg you kick with, look over that respective shoulder. As your opponent approaches, look first and then kick. Once again, as you develop your senses you will be able to tell where your opponent is, kicking first and looking second. This comes after a lot of practice, so for now, the novice should confine his practice to looking and then kicking.

Assume a standing position and imagine that your opponent is behind you.

Cock the foot up in front by raising the knee.

Bend forward slightly and extend the leg back striking with the heel of the foot.

Retract the foot back immediately and plant it down.

Side Snap Or Knife Edge

(1) Assume a neutral bow position, right leg back to 6:00, hands are in Three Shields.

(2) Cock the front left foot in, as if you are going into a one leg stance.

(3) Strike out with the side of the foot and shift your hips as you do the kick so that the back part of your foot makes contact. Think of a chop with the hand. You wouldn't strike with the fingers, and neither do you want to kick with the side of the toes.

(4) Retract the foot, again faster than you strike out.

(5) Plant the foot down.

Assume a neutral bow with the right leg back to 6:00 and the hands in a Three Shields position.

Cock the front left foot in as if you are assuming a one-legged stance.

Strike out with the side of the foot and shift your hips as you strike out. This brings the back part of the foot into contact with the target.

Retract the foot immediately, faster than the strike.

Plant the foot down.

Variation

(1) You can also use the back foot for this technique out of a neutral bow.
(2) Pivot on the front foot as you cock the rear leg up in position and
(3-5) follow the same procedure as above.

You can also use the back of the foot for this technique. This kick is executed from the neutral bow.

Pivot on the front foot as you cock the rear leg up into position.

Strike out with the edge of the foot and shift your hips as you execute the kick to allow the back of the foot to make contact.

Retract the foot immediately.

Plant the foot down into a neutral bow.

Roundhouse

(1) Assume a neutral bow position, right leg back to 6:00, hands are in the Three Shields.

(2) Pivot the front left foot slightly forward, while bringing the right knee across your body pointing it towards the target.

(3) As the knee reaches a point even with the opposite hip, extend the leg out striking with the ball of the foot or with the top of the foot.

(4) Retract the leg even faster than it strikes out.

(5) Plant the foot back into a neutral bow and pivot the front foot back into position.

Assume a neutral bow with the right leg back to 6:00 and the hands in a Three Shields position.

Pivot on the front left foot slightly in a forward manner while bringing the right knee across your body aiming it at the target.

As the knee reaches a point even with the opposite hip, extend the leg out striking the target with the ball of the foot.

Retract the leg faster than the strike.

Plant the foot back down into a neutral bow stance.

Variation

(1) Assume a neutral bow,

(2) step the rear foot to the front foot with a little hopping action,

(3) bring the left leg up with the knee across the body,

(4) extend the foot out striking your target with either the ball or top of the foot.

(5) Retract the foot and

(6) plant it back into position.

Assume a neutral bow stance.

Step the rear foot to the front foot with a little hopping movement.

Bring the left leg up with the knee across the body.

Extend the foot out striking at the target with either the ball or top of the foot.

Retract the foot immediately.

Plant the foot back into position.

(1) Assume a neutral bow, right foot back to 6:00, hands are in the Three Shields.

(2) Step from the front toe-back heel neutral bow to a front heel-back toe position by moving the left foot to 12:00 1:00.

(3) Turn and look over your right shoulder as you draw the right foot up, plant on the ball of the foot, and prepare to kick.

(4) Bend forward slightly and extend the right leg to the rear, striking your opponent with the heel.

(5) Retract the foot,

(6) plant the left foot back and crossout.

Assume a neutral bow position with the right foot back to 6:00 and the hands in a Three Shields position.

Step from the front toe-back heel neutral bow position to a front heel-back toe position by moving the left foot to 12:00 or 1:00.

Turn and look over your right shoulder as you draw the right foot up. Plant down on the ball of the foot and prepare to kick.

Bend forward slightly and extend the right leg to the rear striking the target with the heel.

Retract the foot.

Plant the left foot back and cross-out.

Front Knee

This strike is used for a close infighting situation where you cannot kick. It could be used to strike many different targets. Mainly, the strike would go to the groin but could also strike the face from various positions.

(1) Assume a neutral bow,

(2) bring the right knee straight up to the target.

This strike can be increased in power by using the hands to pull the target towards the knee, so rather than striking a stationary target you are hitting a target moving towards you and doubling your striking power.

Assume the neutral bow position with the right foot back to 6:00 and the hands in a Three Shields position.

Bring the right knee straight up into the target.

Plant the foot back down again.

Roundhouse Knee

(1) Assume a standing position in a close position to your opponent or neutral bow.

(2) Bring the knee across your body as you did when doing the roundhouse kick, but you will strike at the point when you reach the opposite hip.

(3) Retract the knee and plant down.

Assume a neutral bow position with the right foot back to 6:00 and the hands in a Three Shields position.

Bring the knee across the body to strike.

Retract the knee back and plant down.

PUNCHES

Punches are methods of striking your opponent with your fists. Practice the different methods of delivering these punches and you will be ready for any situation. Punch strong on the thrust punches but whip the snap punches as fast as you can, create an explosion at the end of the snap and you will generate more power than the thrusts.

Straight Snap

(1) To practice these first four punches start out in a square horse.

(2) As the hand moves forward your palm is up until the elbow passes by your body and

(3) then the hand begins to turn over until the palm is down. Strike with the first two knuckles of the hand. By doing this you have all the bones in your hand and arm in alignment. Keep the wrist straight.

(4) Retract the hand back in the same path it traveled out. Turning the hand like this at the point of impact creates a torquing action that increases the power as well as creating a tearing action on impact.

(5) Cock back to hip.

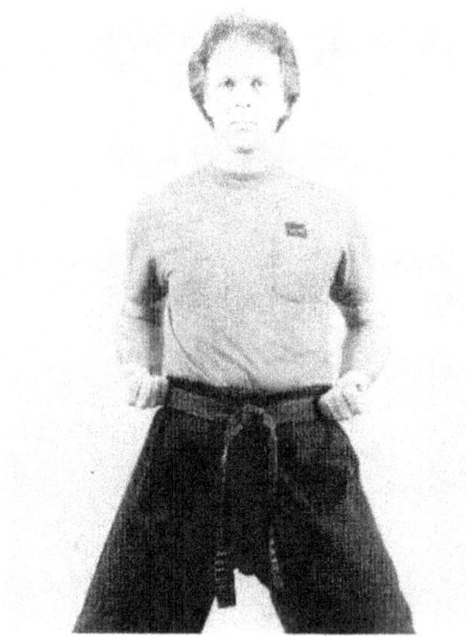

Assume a square horse stance.

As the hand moves forward, your palm is up until the elbow passes the body.

The hand turns over until the palm is facing downwards. Strike with the first two knuckles of the fist.

Retract the hand back in the same path.

Cock the fist back to the hip.

Straight Thrust

In our system a snapping punch means that you retract the punch back faster than you strike out. Once again this creates explosive power at the point of impact. On the other hand, a thrust punch is a driving type of power. The punch is left out in an extended position until the next punch is delivered.

(1) Assume a square horse,

(2) As the hand moves forward your palm is up until your elbow passes by your body and

(3) then your hand begins to turn over until the palm is down. You strike with the first two knuckles of the hand.

(4) Retract when the next punch is delivered, thus creating cross pulling power. The key here is on the second punch, you retract the first one as the second is being delivered. Upon impact with the second punch, the first one has been cocked back to the hip. The cross pulling motion creates and increases the force on the second punch. You can tell the difference yourself in the power of the first and second punches.

Assume a square horse stance.

As the hand moves forward, your palm is up until the elbow passes by your body.

The hand turns over until it is facing downwards. Strike with the first two knuckles of the fist.

Retract the first hand as you begin to deliver the second punch.

The first hand cocks to the hip as the second hand makes contact with the target.

Vertical Snap

(1) Assume a square horse.

(2) As the hand moves forward your palm is up until your elbow passes by your body and

(3) then the hand begins to turn over until it is in a vertical position. Strike with the first two knuckles of the hand.

(4) Retract the hand back on the same path it traveled out.

(5) Cock to the hip.

Assume a square horse stance.

As the hand moves forward, your palm is up until the elbow passes by the body.

Then, the hand begins to turn over until the palm is facing in a vertical position. Strike with the first two knuckles of the hand.

Retract the hand back in the same path.

Cock the fist to the hip.

Vertical Thrust

(1) Assume a square horse.

(2) As the hand moves forward, your palm is up until your elbow passes by your body.

(3) Then, the hand begins to turn over until the palm is vertical. Strike with the first two knuckles of the hand as in the previous examples.

For a punching drill, do these four punches as a four count punching exercise. Right and left, first executing the snap punches and then the thrust punches.

(4) Retract the first hand as you begin to deliver the second punch.

(5) The first hand cocks to the hip as the second hand makes contact with the target.

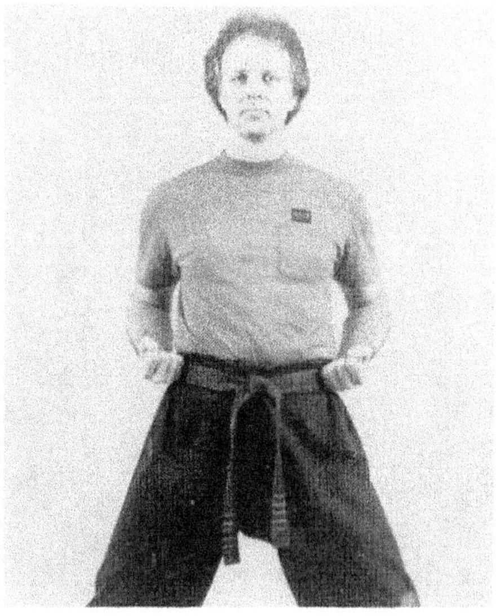

Assume a square horse stance.

As the hand moves forward, your palm is up until the elbow passes by your body.

The hands begins to turn over until the palm is in a vertical position to strike.

Retract the first hand as you begin to deliver the second punch.

The first hand cocks to your hip as the second hand makes contact with the target.

Shuffle

This is a total technique and not just a punch for many different types of punches can be delivered out of the "shuffle" position.

(1) Assume a neutral bow, right leg back to 6:00, hands are in Three Shields.

(2) The front foot steps forward as in the attack pattern, deliver a straight snap punch to the opponent's body.

(3) Shuffle the back foot up to a position on the ball of the foot and retract your punch back. As you are shuffling into position your hips and upper body turn forward, throwing your body behind the punch.

(4) Plant the foot back to a neutral bow.

Assume a neutral bow stance with the right leg back to 6:00 and the right hand cocked to the hip.

The front foot steps forward in an attack pattern. Deliver a straight snap punch to the opponent's body. One variation would be to deliver a vertical snap punch to the face.

Shuffle the back foot up to a position on the ball of the foot and retract the fist back to the hip.

Plant the foot back to a neutral bow.

Leopard

(1) Assume a neutral bow and do this technique from the shuffle position. Cock the rear hand to the chest in a half fist by bending the fingers down. You will be striking with the second knuckles of the fingers. This strike has the throat as its target but by varying the position of the hand you can strike any of the other softer targets.

(2) On the step, extend the arm as if doing a straight snap punch. The difference being that you are striking with a half fist.

(3) Finish the shuffle by moving the rear foot into position and retract the punch back.

(4) Shift back to a neutral bow.

Assume a neutral bow stance with the right foot back to 6:00 and the right hand cocked in a half-fist high around chest level.

On the step, extend the arm as in a straight
snap punch.

Finish the shuffle by moving the rear foot
into position and retract the punch.

Shift back to a neutral bow position.

Vertical Dragon Head

(1) Assume a neutral bow, and do this punch out of a shuffle position. To form the dragon head Fist, make a fist in a vertical position, extend your middle knuckle by using your thumb to push out the finger which will give you added strength on the strike. This strike goes to the armpit, solar plexus, throat, temple or any other soft target.

(2) On the step, extend the arm out as if you are doing a vertical snap, except your middle knuckle will be extended. Strike to the solar plexus.

(3) Finish the shuffle and retract the punch.

(4) Shift back to a neutral bow.

For another application see clutching feathers in the self-defense technique section.

Assume a neutral bow stance with the right foot back to 6:00 and the right hand cocked in a vertical fist position with the middle knuckle extended. The thumb can be used for added strength by placing it behind the knuckle. The hand should be cocked high to the chest.

On the step, extend the arm as if doing a
vertical snap punch.

Finish the shuffle and retract the punch
back.

Shift back to a neutral bow stance.

SPECIAL WEAPONS

Special weapons as they are called in our style, are methods of striking with either the open hand, in a palm strike or chop or with the elbow. It usually covers anything not included in the punch catagory. Presented here are fifteen palm, chop and elbow strikes. These will give you the versatility to take you beyond the novice stage.

Straight Palm

(1) Assume a neutral bow with the rear hand cocked high to the chest in a variation of the leopard punch. This time you will be striking with the heel palm. The palm should be facing out as if it were cocked to the hip. As you strike, turn the palm over in the same manner as punching thus giving your strike a torquing action. This strike is done in a snapping motion.

(2) From your neutral bow, shift forward to a forward bow timing your straight palm to reach your opponent's chin at the same time your hips reach their maximum forward position.

(3) Shift back to a neutral bow retracting your palm to your chest. As you strike forward, your lead parry hand retracts to a secondary position. Then, as you retract your strike, extend your parry back out to the original three shields position. This strike is usually directed to the chin, jaw or the nose area. It is a very powerful strike and I have seen an opponent lifted off the ground when struck directly on the chin. The cross pulling action of the strike and parry generates the added power and also affords you the protection if in a vulnerable striking position. A general rule to remember is that whenever you strike out the secondary hand becomes a parry and is pulled back close to your body. Whenever you strike high, parry low to the open area or when striking low, parry high again to the open area. In this manner, you are always covered.

Assume a neutral bow stance with the right leg back to 6:00. Cock the right hand high to the chest as in a variation of the leopard punch.

Shift forward to a forward bow and execute a straight palm strike to your opponent's chin.

Shift back to a neutral bow retracting the palm to your chest.

Inward Chop

(1) In a standing position,

(2) step the right foot forward to 12:00, raising the hand to your shoulder.

(3) As your foot plants, strike with the edge of your right hand to your opponent's collar bone, neck or throat area. The left hand is moving up to parry in front of your body at the same instant the strike lands.

Try this strike without the use of the parry and the cross pulling action it generates. Then do it with the parry and the cross pulling action. You will see the difference in the power of the strike plus the added benefit of the parry for defense.

Start from a standing position.

Step the right foot forward to 12:00 raising the hand to your shoulder.

As your foot plants, strike with the edge of your right hand to your opponent's collar bone, neck or throat. The left hand parries in front of the body.

Outward Whipping Chop

(1) Assume a neutral bow, with the right foot forward. The left hand parries in front of your face and the right hand is cocked to the left ear across the body in preparation for the strike.

(2) Shift your front heel forward to a reverse bow as you extend the right hand out, chopping to the bridge of the nose, the throat or the side of the neck.

(3) Retract the hand back and shift back to a neutral bow.

The shifting to a reverse bow and the whipping action of this technique give it its power. Once again, try this technique without the shift, just remain in a neutral bow. I think you will see the difference not only in power but also in the speed of delivery. For an example in a self-defense situation, refer to the lone kimono.

Assume a neutral bow stance with the left foot back to 6:00. The left and parries in front of the face and the right hand is cocked to the left ear across the body in preparation for the strike.

Shift to a reverse bow as you extend the right hand out, chopping to the bridge of the nose, the throat, or the side of the neck.

Retract the hand and shift back to a neutral bow.

Back Hammerfist

(1) In a standing position keep your hands at your sides.

(2) With an opponent behind you, step back with the right foot to 6:00, neutral bow, strike with the same part of the hand as you chop with. Only difference is that your hand is closed. Again, as you step back and strike, parry with the left hand over your right shoulder. The parry, in this instance, can be used in a dual manner. If someone was grabbing your right shoulder and turning you around to punch you, your left parry could deflect that oncoming punch while you strike. Also, if you catch them before they launch their attack you can use it as an eye poke over the shoulder. See obscure wing or crushing hammer in the self-defense technique section for an example.

(3) Another way to practice this technique is to assume a neutral bow, hands are in Three Shields.

(4) Shift to a reverse bow, your front hand circles down and strikes the opponent to the groin. The rear hand parries high covering the open area. You have cross pulling hand action plus the added power of the shift to reverse bow. A very powerful strike.

Assume a standing position with your hands at your sides.

Step back with the right foot to 6:00 in a neutral bow position and strike to the groin with the bottom of your fist. The left hand parries over the right shoulder.

Underhand Reverse Hammerfist

"Underhand" refers to the target which, in this case, is the groin. The reverse part of the hammerfist is the opposite side of the fist.

(1) From a neutral bow position, the right foot steps back to 6:00 with the hands in a Three Shields position.

(2) Take a shuffle step forward to 12:00 with your right foot (to a shuffle position). Strike with the right underhand reverse hammerfist to the groin. The left hand parries in front of the chest.

(3) The right foot steps back into a neutral bow position.

This technique can be done in the shuffle position using the rear hand to strike for a variation in this technique.

Assume a neutral bow stance with the right foot back to 6:00 and the hands in a Three Shields position.

Execute a shuffle step forward to 12:00 with your right foot to a shuffle position.

Strike with the right fist (reverse hammer-fist) to the groin. The left hand parries the front of the chest.

Step the right foot back to a neutral bow position.

Overhead Hammerfist

(1) From a standing position,

(2) take a step forward to 12:00, neutral bow, circle your right hand overhead and

(3) strike to the top of your opponent's head or the bridge of the nose. The left hand will parry in front of the chest.

To perform the three hammerfist techniques as a drill begin

(1) by stepping back to 6:00 with the right foot and strike with the right back hammerfist.

(2) Next, step the right foot forward to 12:00, strike with the right underhand reverse hammerfist.

(3) Circle your right hand and strike with the overhead hammerfist. Repeat for the left side.

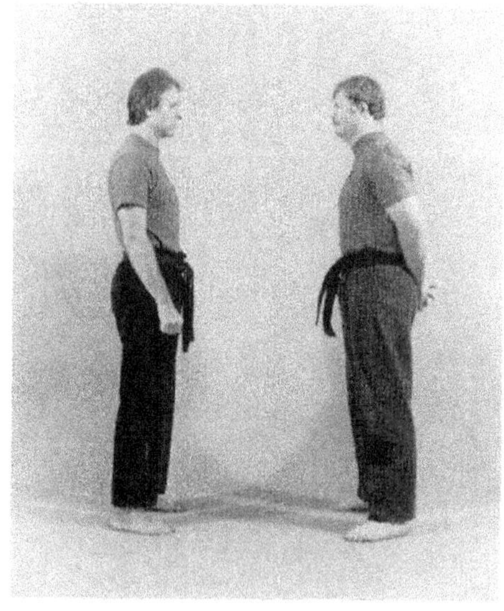

Assume a standing position.

Take a step forward to 12:00 to a neutral bow position and circle your right hand overhead.

Strike to the top of your opponent's head. The left hand parries in front of the chest.

Inward Elbow

(1) From a standing position,

(2) step the right foot forward to 12:00 neutral bow, right arm cocked parallel to the ground with your fist close to your chest.

(3) As the foot plants down, impact should be made with the forearm part of the elbow. If you strike to the face, parry low to protect your chest area. When striking to the chest parry to the face.

This strike can be done in a raking manner or like a thrust punch driving straight through the target.

For an example of the raking method, see the triggered salute and for the thrusting method, see the gift of destruction in the self-defense technique section.

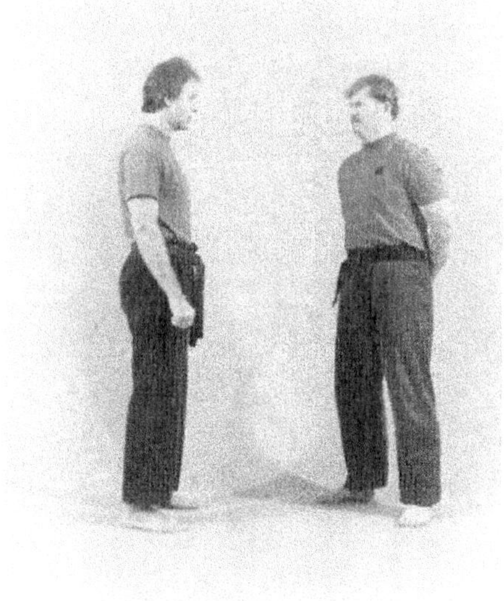

Assume a standing position.

Step the right foot forward to 12:00 into a neutral bow position with the right arm cocked parallel to the ground with your fist close to your chest.

As the foot plants down, impact should be made with the forearm area near the elbow.

Outward Elbow

(1) From a standing position

(2) take a step out to 3:00 raising the arm parallel in front of your body.

(3) As you plant your foot to 3:00, strike with the back of the elbow. Again, this strike can be directed to the face or the ribs.

We very often use this in conjunction with a raking inward elbow. See triggered salute in the self-defense technique section.

Assume a standing position.

Take a step out to 3:00 raising the arm parallel in front of your body.

As you plant your foot, strike with the back of the elbow and parry low to the rib-cage area.

Back Elbow

(1) In a standing position,
(2) either step out to 3:00 or back to 6:00 with the right foot. As you do, cock the right hand to your hip as if to prepare for a punch. Strike with the back part of the elbow to your opponent's solar plexus. Parry with the left hand over your right shoulder. See obscure wing in the self-defense technique section.

Start from a standing position.

Step out to 3:00 into a square horse position. Cock the right hand to your hip as if to prepare for a punch; strike with the back of the elbow to your opponent's solar plexis. Parry with the left hand over your right shoulder.

Obscure Back Elbow

This strike is usually done in conjunction with either a back elbow or a back hammerfist catching the opponent under the chin.

(1) In a standing position, one of the other strikes can be delivered as the opponent bends forward. Your palm faces him towards the rear.

(2) Step out to 3:00 into a square horse and cock the right hand to prepare to strike.

(3) Drive the elbow straight up under the chin.

(4) Retract the fist back immediately.

For an example, refer to the obscure wing in the self-defense section of this book.

A good drill for the four different elbow strikes is as follows:

(1) Step the right foot forward to 12:00 into a neutral bow. Do a right inward elbow.

(2) Right outward elbow.

(3) Step the right foot back to 6:00 into a neutral bow. Do a right back elbow.

(4) Do a right obscure elbow. Repeat on the opposite side.

From a standing position, your palm should be facing the opponent to the rear.

Step out to 3:00 into a square horse and cock
the right hand to strike.

Drive the elbow straight up under the chin.

Retract back immediately.

Inward Overhead Elbow

(1) Double your opponent over with a kick to the stomach or groin.

(2) Check his hand.

(3) Step forward, circle the right hand from the outside, inwards and overhead. Strike down with the bottom part of the elbow. The palm is facing yourself. The strike is directed to the back along the spine or kidney area. This is a finishing technique and not meant to be a first move in a series of moves. Parry to the unprotected area.

After you double your opponent over with a kick to the stomach or groin.

Check his hand as you step forward. Circle the right hand from the outside in an inward direction overhead.

Strike down with the bottom part of the elbow. The palm is facing yourself.

Outward Overhead Elbow

(1) With the opponent bent over along side of you,

(2) step out to 3:00 with the right foot, circle the right hand from the inside across your body, overhead in an outward manner.

(3) Strike with the bottom part of the elbow, palm facing you and parrying to the open area.

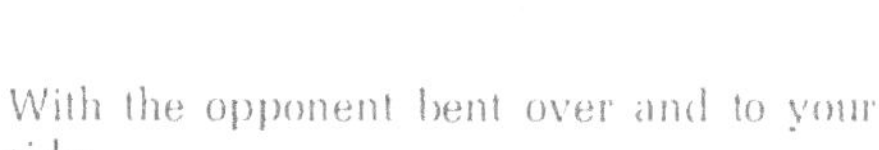

With the opponent bent over and to your side.

Step out to 3:00 with the right foot and circle your right hand from the inside across your body in an outward manner to an overhead position. Strike with the bottom part of the elbow. The palm is facing yourself.

Inward Horizontal Pressure Rake

This technique is used for a clothes grab and can be seen in the self-defense technique section, referring to the lone kimono.

(1) Your opponent is grabbing your shirt with his left hand and after an initial strike to the elbow you pin his hand to your chest with your left hand.

(2) Strike with a right hammerfist forearm strike on the top of his forearm about two inches from the elbow on the nerve center. This causes a shock to shoot down the arm and make him open his hand. To insure that the pain travels down the forearm to the hand,

(3) rake your forearm from the target back toward your body, pulling your opponent into you at the same time.

Your opponent grabs your shirt with his left hand. After an initial strike to the elbow, pin his head to your chest with your left hand. Cock your right hand to your shoulder.

Strike with a right hammer-fist forearm strike to the top of his forearm.

Rake your forearm from the target back towards your own body.

Downward Vertical Elbow

This technique is used as a secondary or finishing strike for a front headlock and can be seen in the self-defense technique section, locking horns.

(1) After breaking the hold and with the elbow pointing up in a vertical position in front of the body,

(2) take a short step forward and strike straight down to the sternum or solar plexus. If the opponent is bent back farther, strike with the forearm part of the elbow.

After breaking the hold, the elbow is positioned upwards in front in a vertical position.

Take a short step forward and strike straight down to the sternum or solar plexis. Strike with the front of the elbow.

Double Underhand Thumb Fist

To make a thumb fist, close the hand as you would to make a fist. Instead of having your thumb in front of your knuckles move it to the top of your index finger. White Crane kung-fu uses this fist so that they can punch with any side of the fist. Underhand should tell you that the strike is going to the groin area.

(1) This particular strike is for a front bear hug with your arms pinned, an example can be seen in the self-defense technique section, thrusting prongs.

(2) As you step back with the right foot, strike to the groin with both thumb fists.

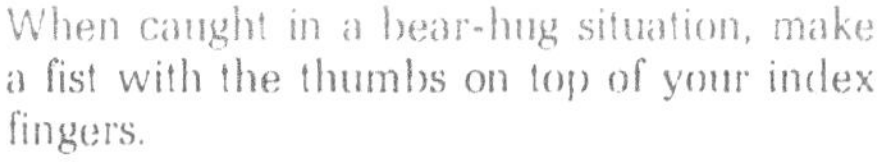

When caught in a bear-hug situation, make a fist with the thumbs on top of your index fingers.

As you step back with the right foot, strike to the groin with both thumb fists.

FINGER TECHNIQUES

Finger techniques differ from the strikes in that they are methods of clawing, poking and whipping with the fingers. In this level, you have an example of each method.

Straight Thrust

(1) Assume a square horse with your hands cocked to the hips to practice this technique. There are four different ways to deliver this strike. The method of delivery is the same as a straight thrust punch.

(2) As your hand leaves the hip, your first two fingers extend.

(3) As the elbow passes by the body turn the hand over from its palm up position to palm down. The final turn of the palm comes right before impact, in this case the eye or the throat right above the collar bone. For an example of a straight thrust to the throat see self-defense technique section, thrusting leaves.

The four ways of delivering this strike are:

(4) two fingers striking one eye or throat;

(5) two fingers striking both eyes;

(6) all four fingers separated at the middle and ring fingers, two fingers to each eye

(7) or all four fingers striking both eyes.

This is the snake's tongue technique with various methods of striking.

Assume a square horse stance and cock your hands to your hips.

As your hand leaves the hip, extend the first two fingers outwards.

As the elbow passes by the body, turn the hand over into a palm-down position. Both fingers strike one eye or the throat area.

A variation with the fingers striking both eyes.

A variation with four fingers striking both eyes.

A variation with four fingers striking both eyes. Two fingers in each eye.

Outward Whip

The whip is derived from the crane and can be delivered from an open handed Three Shields position or from a crane's beak position. I think the more practical and quicker method will be to assume a:

(1) neutral bow with the hands open in a Three Shields position. The whip is done by whipping the hand at the wrist, much the same way you would snap a towel. The back of the hand strikes to the nose and as you retract immediately the fingers whip across the eyes.

(2) Take a short step forward with the front foot as if you are beginning the attack pattern. As the foot plants the strike should land.

(3) Retract back to neutral bow, Three Shields position.

Assume a neutral bow stance with the left foot back to 6:00 and the hands are in an open Three Shields position. The whip is accomplished by whipping the hand at the wrist. The back of the hand strikes to the nose and retracts immediately as the fingers whip across the eyes.

Take a short step forward with the front foot and strike as the foot plants down.

Retract back to a neutral bow position and pull back your hand immediately.

Overhead Claw

(1) Practice this technique in a square horse, hands cocked to the hip.

(2) Circle the right hand overhead,

(3) come down from top to bottom across your opponent's face. This is a tiger's claw so when you strike think of the strength and speed of the tiger when performing this movement.

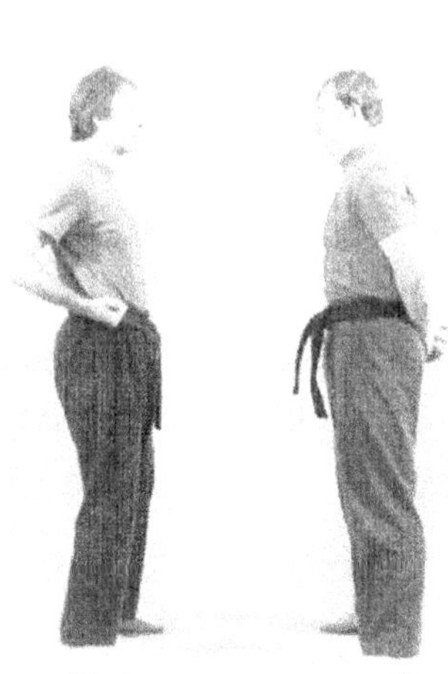

Begin in a square horse position with the hands cocked to the hips.

Circle the right hand overhead.

Strike down across your opponent's face.

SPECIALITY TECHNIQUES

These are called speciality techniques because they are not practiced in the same manner as the other techniques are. They are practiced, usually, in the context of a self-defense technique. I chose to call them out individually so that you can see exactly how they are performed.

Breaks: Inward/Outward

(1) Assume a standing position, as your opponent pushes you with his right hand,

(2) step forward with your left foot to about 11:00, strike a left inward block at the elbow and catch their arm at the wrist by blocking back toward yourself with your right hand. This is very much like a reverse inward block. Timing and the amount of pressure will determine the difference between a strained or broken elbow.

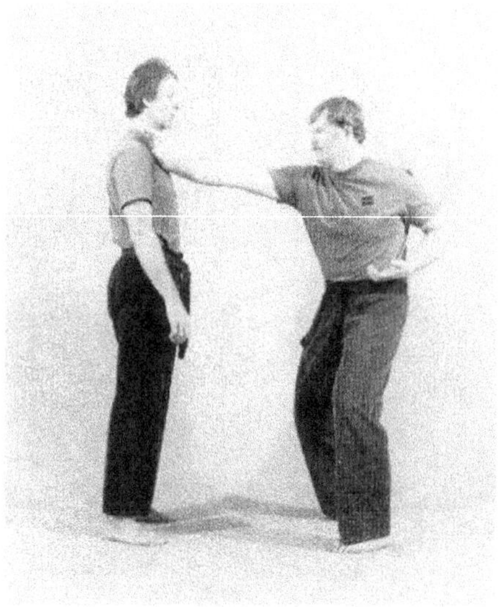

Assume a standing position as your opponent tries to push you with his right hand.

Step forward with your left foot to 11:00 and strike with a left inward block to the elbow and catch his arm at the wrist, blocking back towards yourself with your right hand.

Inward At The Elbow

(1) Assume your opponent has you in a cross hand grab, where he is grabbing your right hand with his right hand.

(2) Turn your right hand straight up as if you were starting to brush your hair back. As your hand gets to about waist height, you are stepping forward with your left foot to about 11:00 neutral bow,

(3) Turn your wrist and grab your opponent's hand with an eagle talon.

(4) At the same time, lock the hold down on the wrist with a slight jerk and strike a left inward block at the elbow.

Your opponent has you in a cross hand grab with the opponent's right hand grasping your right hand.

Turn your right hand straight upwards as if brushing your hair back. As your hand reaches the height of your wrist, step forward with your left foot to about 11:00 assuming a neutral bow position.

Turn your opponent's wrist and grab his hand with an eagle talon claw.

At the same time, lock the hold down on the wrist with a slight jerk and strike with a left inward block at the elbow.

Take Down: Inward Elbow

(1) In the circumstance where the opponent has extended his right arm.
(2) Grab the right wrist with your left hand.
(3) Step the right foot forward to 11:00 behind the opponent's lead foot.
(4) Strike to the chest with an inward elbow.
(5) Shift to a forward bow.
(6) Take the opponent down.

In the situation where the opponent extends his arm to grab your arm.

Grab the right wrist with your left hand.

Step with the right foot forward to about 11:00 behind the opponent's lead foot.

Strike the chest with an inward elbow thrust.

Shift to a forward bow.

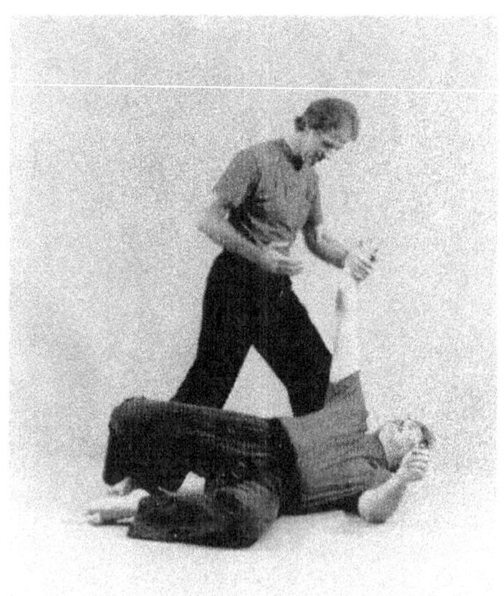

Take the opponent down by upsetting his balance.

Fall: Backwards

(1) When you are caught off-guard and are pushed, you are falling back.

(2) Try to sit as close to the ground as you can.

(3) Just before you hit the ground, strike the palms on the ground to break the fall.

(4) Tuck your head forward (keeping the chin in) and roll back.

(5) Keep one leg across your groin and the other leg ready to kick. The hands are in the Three Shields position.

When you are caught off guard and pushed down.

Start to fall back.

Try to sit as close to the ground as possible just before you hit. Hit the ground with your elbows to break the fall.

Tuck your chin in and roll back and keep one leg crossed and the other leg ready to kick if necessary.

FORMS

Short 1 Blocking Set

Salutation. Left palm push down.

Right downward block.

Left inside downward palm down.

Right inside downward palm up.

Step right foot back to 6:00, neutral bow, left inward block.

Step left foot back to 6:00, neutral bow, right upward block.

Step right foot back to 6:00, neutral bow, left extended outward block.

Step left foot to your right and out to 9:00, face 3:00, neutral bow, left inward parry, right outward block.

Draw the right foot back to a cat stance, right downward parry, left inward parry.

Shift your weight to the right foot, turn and face 12:00, step the left foot forward, left cat stance, left downward parry, right inward parry.

Step the left foot out to 9:00, square horse, left inward parry, right hand cocks to your hip.

Shift to 9:00, forward bow, right palm push down, left hand cocks to hip.

Reverse bow facing 9:00,

Step the right foot up, face 3:00, one leg stance.

Hop to the right leg, face 12:00, one leg stance.

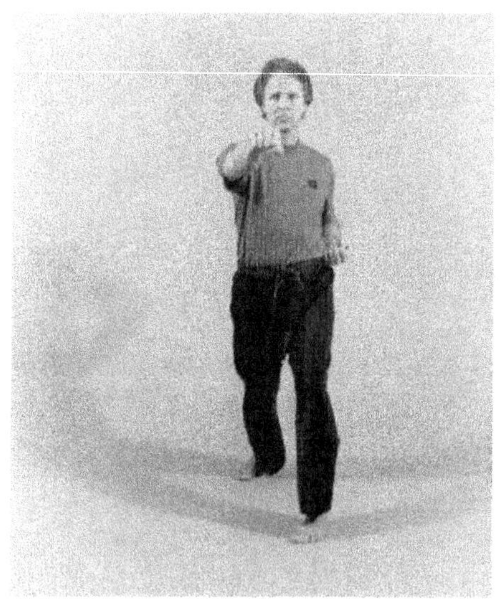

Step the left foot forward to 12:00, shift to forward bow, right straight thrust punch.

Neutral bow, left vertical snap punch, right hand parries to left ribs.

Shift to Three Shields, right front snap kick, plant forward.

Left front snap kick, plant out to 9:00, square horse.

Square Horse, Three Shields.

Right Inside Downward Parry.

Left Inside Downward Parry.

Left Inward Parry.

Right Outward Parry.

Right Inward Block.

Right Inward Parry.

Left Outward Parry.

Left Inside Downward Parry, Palm Up.

Right Inward Block.

Left Upward Block.

Right Extended Outward Block.

Left Outward Block.

Salutation.
The left foot steps back to 6:00 into a neutral bow. Execute a right inward block.

The right foot steps back to 6:00 into a neutral bow. Execute a left inward block.

The right foot steps to the left and out to 3:00 into a neutral bow. Now facing 9:00, execute a right inward parry and a left outward block.

The left foot steps back to 3:00 into a neutral bow. Execute a right outward block.

Cover with the right foot and face 3:00 into a neutral bow. Execute a left upward block.

The left foot steps back to 9:00 into a neutral bow. Right upward block.

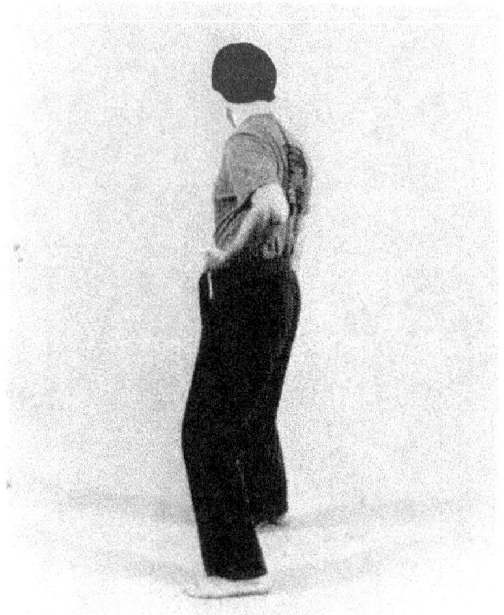

The left foot steps to the right and back to 12:00 into a neutral bow. Facing 6:00, execute a right downward block.

The right foot steps back to 12:00 into a neutral bow. Execute a left downward block.

The left foot steps to the right and out to 9:00 into a square horse stance. Count, "one thousand one" to yourself.

The right foot steps back to 6:00 into a neutral bow. Execute a left inward block.

The left foot steps back to 6:00 into a neutral bow. Execute a right inward block.

The left foot steps to the right and out to 9:00 into a neutral bow. Facing 3:00, execute a left inward parry and a right outward block.

The right foot steps back to 9:00 into a neutral bow. Execute a left outward block.

Cover with the left foot and face 9:00 in a neutral bow position. Execute a right upward block.

The right foot steps back to 3:00 into a neutral bow. Execute a left upward block.

The right foot steps to the left and back to 12:00 into a neutral bow. Facing 6:00, execute a left downward block.

The left foot steps back to 12:00 into a neutral bow. Execute a right downward block.

The right foot steps to the left and out to 3:00 into a square horse stance.

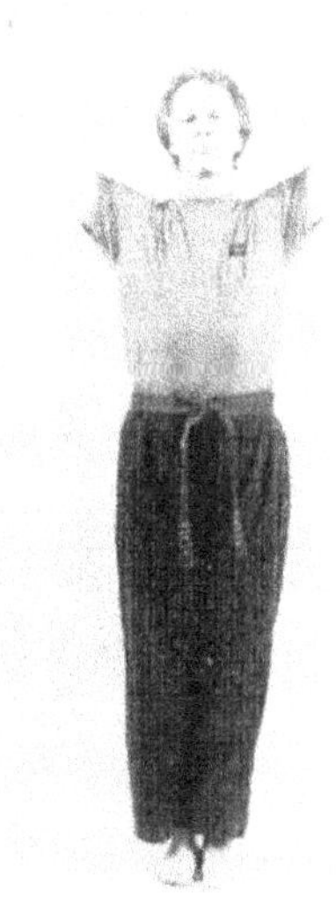

Up into position.

Finish.

Beginner Staff Set-Right Side

Stand with the feet together facing the opponent at 12:00. The staff is held in both hands and is positioned parallel to the ground. Divide the staff into three equal parts with the position of the hands.

Salutation. Execute a left inward block.

Right inward block.

The right foot steps out to 3:00 into a square horse stance. Return staff to center position.

Left inward strike.

Right inward strike.

Left overhead strike.

Right underhand strike.

Left inward strike.

Right inward strike.

Left inward block.

Left outward block.

Left vertical strike.

Right overhead strike to the left side.

The left foot steps over the right into a front twist position. Execute a right overhead inward block.

The right foot steps back to 4:00 into a neutral bow. The staff is held in a ready position.

Beginner Staff Set-Left Side

Stand with your feet together facing 6:00 with the staff held in both hands parallel to the ground. Divide the staff into three equal parts with your hand position.

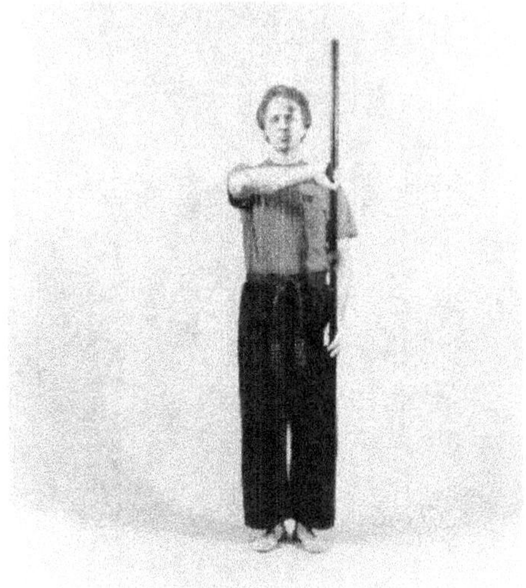

Salutation—A right inward block.

Left inward block.

The left foot steps out to 3:00 into a square horse. The staff moves back to the center position.

Left inward block.

Left outward block.

Upward block.

Downward block.

Left inward block.

Left outward block.

Left inward strike.

Right inward strike.

Left overhead strike to the opponent's head.

As the opponent strikes the staff, move with it circling downwards.

Left outside strike as the left foot steps over the right into a front twist stance.

The right foot steps back to 10:00 into a neutral bow position. The staff is held in a ready position.

Beginner Staff Set-Both Sides Together

Assume stance facing each other. The attacker is facing 12:00 with the feet together. The staff is held with both hands and is parallel to the ground. The defender is facing towards 6:00 in the same manner.
Note: The attacker is on the left and the defender is on the right.

Salutation
Attacker: Right inward block.
Defender: Left inward block.

Attacker: Left inward block.
Defender: Right inward block.

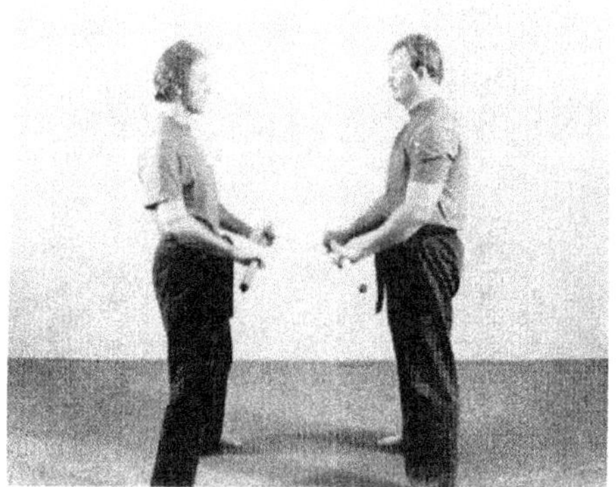

Attacker: The right foot steps out to 3:00 into a square horse, the staff is back to the center position.

Defender: The left foot steps out to 3:00 into a square horse, the staff is back to the center position.

Set
Attacker: Left inward strike.
Defender: Left Inward strike.

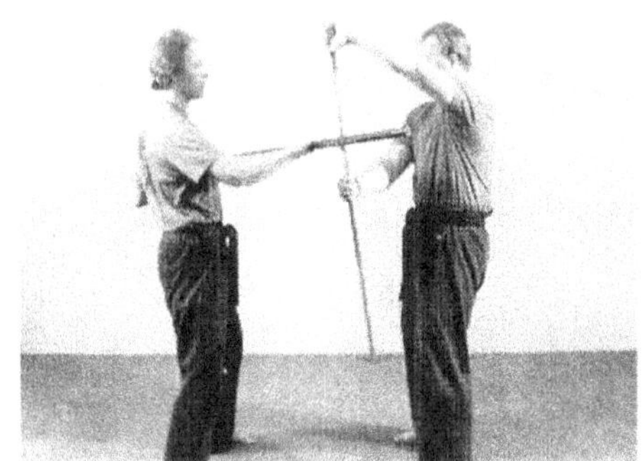

Attacker: Right inward strike.
Defender: Left Outward block.

Attacker: Left overhead strike.
Defender: Upward block.

Attacker: Right underhand strike.
Defender: Downward block.

Attacker: Left inward strike.
Defender: Left inward block.

Attacker: Right inward strike.
Defender: Left outward block.

Attacker: Left inward strike.
Defender: Left inward block.

Attacker: Left outward block.
Defender: Right inward strike.

Attacker: Left vertical strike.
Defender: Left overhead strike to attacker's head.

Attacker: Right overhead strike to the left side.
Defender: Circle down with the striking staff.

Attacker: Step the left foot over the top of the right to a front twist stance executing a right overhead inward block.
Defender: Left outside strike as the left foot steps over the right to a front twist stance.

Attacker: The right foot steps back to 4:00 into a neutral bow with the staff held in a ready position.
Defender: The right foot steps back to 10:00 into a neutral bow with the staff held in a ready position.

Transition to Opposite Side

Attacker: The right foot steps forward to 9:00 into a front twist stance with an upward block.

Defender: The right foot steps forward to 3:00 into a front twist stance with a right overhead strike.

Attacker: The left foot steps forward to 9:00 to the cross position with a downward block.

Defender: The left foot steps forward to 3:00 to the cross position with a left underhand strike.

Attacker: The right foot steps out to 9:00 into a square horse. Facing 6:00, execute a left inward block.

Defender: The right foot steps out to 3:00 into a square horse and facing 12:00 executes a right inward strike.

Attacker: Left inward block.

Defender: Left inward strike.

Attacker: Left outward block.
Defender: Right inward strike.

Attacker: Upward block.
Defender: Left overhead strike.

Attacker: Downward block.
Defender: Right underhand strike.

Attacker: Left inward block.
Defender: Left inward strike.

Attacker: Left outward block.
Defender: Right inward strike.

Attacker: Left inward strike.
Defender: Left inward block.

Attacker: Right inward strike.
Defender: Left outward block.

Attacker: Left overhead strike to the defender's head.
Defender: Left vertical block.

Attacker: Left outside strike as the foot steps over the right into a front twist stance.
Defender: The left foot steps over the top of the right foot to a front twist stance while executing a right overhead inward strike.

Attacker: The right foot steps back to 10:00 into a neutral bow with the staff held in a ready position.
Defender: The right foot steps back to 4:00 into a neutral bow with the staff held in a ready position.

Transition Back to Original
Attacker: The right foot steps forward to 3:00 into a front twist stance with a right overhead strike.
Defender: The right foot steps forward to 9:00 into a front twist stance with an upward block.

Attacker: The left foot steps to 3:00 to the cross position with a left underhand strike.
Defender: The left foot steps forward to 9:00 into a cross position while executing a downward block.

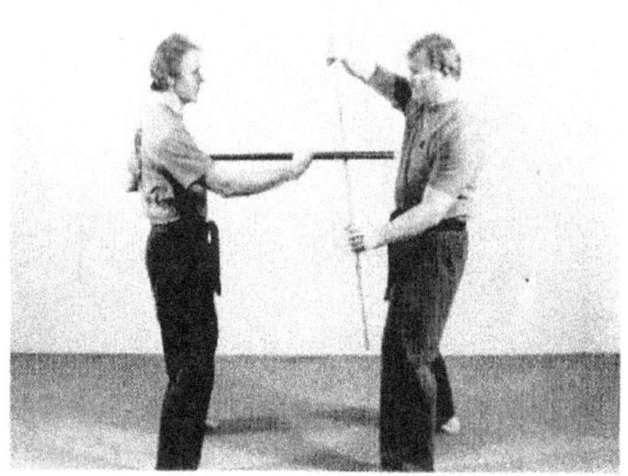

Attacker: The right foot steps out to 3:00 into a square horse. Now facing 12:00, execute a right inward strike.

Defender: The right foot steps out to 9:00 into a square horse. Now facing 6:00, execute a left inward block.

Finishing Salutation

Attacker: Right inward block.
Defender: Right inward block.

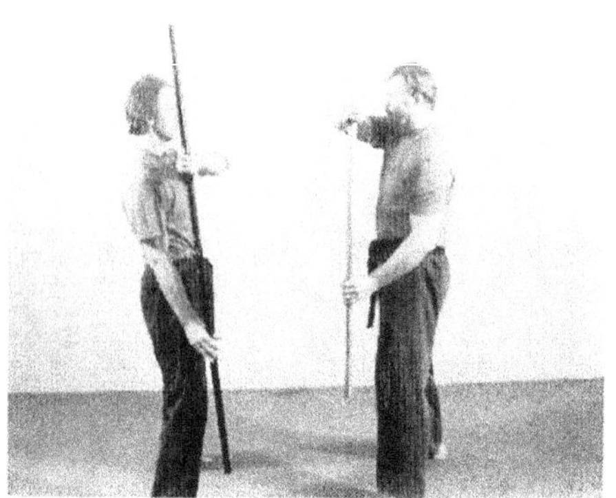

Attacker: Left inward block.
Defender: Right inward block.

Attacker: The right foot steps back to your left with the staff held in front and parallel to the ground.

Defender: The left foot steps back to the right foot and the staff is held in front and parallel to the ground.

SELF-DEFENSE TECHNIQUES

These are a series of blocks, parries and strikes designed to release yourself from any type of hold or committed attack. They involve the most fundamental types of attack. Awareness is enhanced by practicing the defense against these attacks from different and varied angles. These fundamental techniques should inspire you to ponder new ideas and create defenses against other types of attack. These are, by no means, the only techniques to be mastered in Three Shield Kenpo but are a vehicle for greater understanding of the art.

Stand facing your opponent.

As the opponent attacks you, pin his attacking to your left shoulder with your left hand. The right foot steps to about 1:00 into a neutral bow as you deliver a right straight palm to his chin. Allow the force of the attack to turn your body into his movement. It is important to use the opponent's force against himself.

Cock the right hand back to the hip.

A right inward elbow rakes across the solar plexis.

A right outward elbow to the ribs.

Cock the right hand to an outward block by
your right hip.

Execute a right vertical back-knuckle snap
to your opponent's chin.

Cross out retreat to 6:00 or 7:00.

At the end of every situation, be certain to cross out away from your opponent. This gets you out of range of further attack and allows you to size up the situation and make a judgment if further action is required. When a weapon is involved in the attack, be certain that the weapon is removed from the opponent before you cross out.

Lone Kimono-Left Hand Lapel Grab

Stand, facing your opponent.

Your opponent attacks by grabbing your lapel. You must move into action immediately.

The left foot steps back to 6:00 into a neutral bow stance. The left hand pins his hand to the chest and the right hand strikes upward with the top of the forearm to the attacker's elbow.

At the same time, pull the right hand out and cock back to the right shoulder.

Execute a right horizontal pressure rake to the top of his forearm.

Continue to rake across into a cocked position at your left shoulder.

Execute a right outward whipping chop to the opponent's throat and cross out retreat to 6:00 or 7:00.

Thrusting Leaves-Front Choke

Your opponent is choking you with both hands.

The left foot steps back to 6:00 into a neutral bow. Your left hand pins both of the opponent's arms down to your chest. Execute a right straight thrust to his throat area just above the sternum.

Move into a forward bow and execute a left outward chop to the bridge of the opponent's nose. At the same time, the right hand cocks back to the hip.

In a neutral bow position, execute a right upper-cut punch to his solar plexis as the left parries across the top of his arms. You must check the arms to prevent them countering and striking you in the face. Cross out retreat to 6:00 or 7:00.

Evading The Storm-Overhead Club

Stand, facing your opponent.

The opponent steps forward to strike you in an overhead manner with a club. The left foot steps back to 7:00 into a neutral bow stance. Execute a left inward parry deflecting the club hand.

Execute a right extended outward parry.

Grab the club hand.

Execute a right roundhouse kick to the opponent's groin.

Plant your right foot forward into a forward bow stance. Pull the opponent's arm with your right hand to stretch his body off balance. Execute a left straight punch to the lower area of the rib-cage.

Execute a left straight knee to the side of your opponent's thigh area and hop.

Execute a right roundhouse knee to the top
of his thigh area or directly to the groin.

Plant forward while executing a left hip
check block of disturbance. Grab the club
out of his hand as he falls to the ground.
Cross out retreat to 6:00 or 7:00.

Obscure Wing-Left Hand Grabs Your Right Shoulder From The Rear

The opponent is standing directly behind you or off to an angle at 3:00 or 4:00. If he standing at 6:00, step back to 6:00 respectively. Move to the same angle he is attacking and always move into a neutral bow position.

The right foot steps out to 3:00 into a square horse stance. Look over the right shoulder and execute a right back elbow to the opponent's solar plexis. The left hand parries over your right shoulder. Note: If you catch the opponent off guard and he falls forwards, your left hand will poke his eyes rather than parry.

Execute a right hammer fist to your opponent's groin. Turn your palm to face your opponent.

Note: If the opponent attempts to turn you around, your parry will deflect his oncoming blow as you strike him with the other hand.

Execute a right back obscure elbow to his chin. Cross out retreat to 10:00.

Crushing Hammer-Back Bear Grab-Arms Pinned

The opponent has you in a back bear grab with your arms pinned.

The right foot steps out to 3:00 into a square horse stance. The right hand pins your opponent's hands to your chest, the left hand executes a back hammerfist to his groin.

The left foot steps to the right side.

As the left foot moves behind the opponent's right leg into a forward bow. Execute a left back heel palm to his groin.

In a neutral bow position, execute a left back obscure elbow to his chin and simultaneously cock your right fist over your head. This should throw off his arms and eliminate his hold on you.

In a forward bow stance facing your opponent, execute a right downward hammerfist to his groin and the left hand parries to the right side of your own face.

In a neutral bow position, cross out with a strong instep in a sweeping movement to 2:00 to knock him off balance and to the ground.

Locking Horns-Front Headlock

The opponent has you in a headlock with his right forearm across your throat.

The right foot steps to 12:00 into a neutral bow position, the left hand grabs the choking hand of the opponent and the right hand executes a reverse chop to his groin.

Turn the palm to face the opposite direction and execute a right front obscure elbow to his chin.

Take a short step forward with your right foot.

Execute a right downward vertical elbow to his sternum. Cross out retreat to 6:00 or 7:00.

Bending Twin Kimono-Two Hand Lapel Grab

The opponent grabs your lapels with both hands.

The right foot steps forward to 12:00 into a neutral bow position, the left hand pins your opponent's arms to your chest and the right hand executes an upper-cut punch to his solar plexis.

Execute a left outward chop to the bridge of his nose and the right hand cocks back to the hip.

Circle the right hand over your head.

Execute a right hammerfist to the base of the neck. Simultaneously, your left hand parries back over the top of your opponent's arms. Cross out retreat to 6:00 or 7:00.

Thrusting Prongs-Front Bear Grab-Arms Pinned

The opponent has you from the front pinning your arms in a bear hug.

The right foot steps back to 6:00 into a neutral bow. Execute a double underhand thumb fists to his groin.

Grab his hips with both hands.

Pull his body towards yourself and execute a right straight knee to his groin at the same time. Cross out retreat to 5:00 or 6:00.

Clutching Feathers-Left Hand Hair Grab

The opponent grabs your hair with his left hand.

The left foot steps back to 6:00 into a neutral bow position, the left hand pins the opponent's hand to your head. Execute a right vertical dragon head punch to the opponent's left armpit.

The left hand parries the opponent's hand off of the head.

Execute a right extended outward block as your left hand cocks back high to your chest.

In a forward bow stance, execute a left straight palm to his chin and the right block remains up in position.
In a neutral bow position, cross out retreat to 6:00 or 7:00.

Gift of Destruction-Handshake

For an opponent who is trying to hurt you with a handshake in a strong grip.

The left foot steps forward and execute a right straight knee to the opponent's groin. Pull his hand to your right hip and do a left horizontal heel palm strike to his right elbow.

Plant forward into a neutral bow; the left hand parries his right arm down by pushing down on his forearm; execute a right inward elbow to his face. Cross out retreat to 6:00 7:00.

Calming The Storm-Roundhouse Club

Stand, facing your opponent.

The opponent steps forward with his right foot and swings a club at you in a roundhouse manner. The right foot steps forward to 12:00 into a neutral bow, execute a left extended outward block on his arm to block the club and do right vertical punch to his face.

The right hand parries his arm down; do a left vertical punch to his sternum.

Execute a left outward parry with a hook and do a right back-knuckle to his ribs.

Turn your left hand over and grab the club as you cross out retreat to 6:00–7:00.

Twirling Leopard-Left Hand Belt Grab From The Rear

The opponent is behind you.

He grabs your belt with his left hand.

The left foot steps back to 5:00 into a forward bow, execute a left downward block on the hand grabbing your belt and a right straight palm to his chin.

Do a right straight knee to his groin.

Hop and execute a left roundhouse knee to his left inner knee.

Scrape his shins down his left leg and do a left stomp to his left instep. Cross out retreat to 1:00–2:00.

FREE STYLE TECHNIQUES

In an actual fighting situation when it is uncertain what your opponent will do, I again offer a few more ideas. You can practice in a controlled situation what you might have to do for real, some day. Always remember to be spontaneous and flexible in any type of situation. Do not be rigid when you must be supple and quick.

Spinning Branch-Right To Right

Right on right means that both you and your opponent have your right foot forward in a neutral bow or free style fighting position.

The rear leg steps to your front in a forward hopping manner. Execute a right roundhouse kick to the opponent's groin.

Plant down to 10:00.

Execute a left spinning back kick to his body.

Shielding Hammer-Right To Left

The first designation is always yours; therefore, your right foot is forward and your
opponent's left foot is forward.

When your opponent opens his stance much
as a boxer would do, your right foot steps
forward as if beginning the attack pattern;
deflect his lead hand out with a quick outward block.

Execute a right vertical thrust punch to his
face.

Five Swords-Right To Right

You are facing your opponent and both of you have your right foot forward.

Start your attack pattern, step your right foot forward to 12:00, right check block to his lead hand.

Cock the right hand to the left shoulder.

right outward chop to his neck.

Start left foot crossing forward, left straight palm to the side of his face.

As your left foot plants to the cross position, right upper cut punch to his stomach, your left hand is in a lead hand Three Shields position. Step your right foot forward to 12:00, neutral bow, right hand in the lead Three Shields.

You are facing your opponent with your right foot forward against his left foot.

Start the attack pattern, step with the right foot forward to 12:00 and execute a right inward parry.

Left outward parry with a hook on his lead
hand.

Right outward back-knuckle to his ribs.

Start the cross with your left foot and execute a left downward parry on his arm, circle back up and execute a right outward
back-knuckle to his face.

HERBS

I began my herb training on January 5, 1972. I know this because it was three days before my daughter Brandi's third birthday and she was scheduled to have her tonsils out. My brother, Terry, and his friend, Neil, had hitchhiked in from Missouri and were staying with us for a few days. We were talking about the operation and Neil was concerned about it and brought up an interesting point which made me think. He said if you are going to build a race car you wouldn't go to a junk yard to find out how to and you don't necessarily go to a doctor to stay healthy. Most of the time they have to deal with effects rather than causes. He suggested that I check with a good health food store and see if there was a natural way to correct the problem.

Terry had given me three or four books on herbs so I began to research this and found one herb which would cure tonsilitis. I went to the health food store, I always dealt with, and the girl who worked there at the time was studying medicine, specializing in eyes, ears, nose and throat. She was very excited when I told her what I wanted to do. She suggested that I read *Back to Eden* by Jethro Kloss. I looked through the book and reconfirmed the facts about the herb in question and I added another one to it. The next day I brought Brandi in so that she could see the swollen state of her tonsils. Ten days later I brought Brandi back in to the store, completely healed. Her tonsils had reduced to normal size and the infection was gone. The girl couldn't believe the results, for although she believed herbs would work, she had never actually witnessed it personally.

That was my first experiment with herbs and I started with two herbs, golden seal and myrrh gum powder. I made a tea with the golden seal which Brandi drank three times a day and a gargle made with golden seal and myrrh. She gargled three–four times a day.

The fact that they were going to operate on Brandi to remove her tonsils did not necessarily make this situation a critical one. The doctor thought it could relieve the sore throat problems she constantly had. In an emergency situation, I would always consult a medical doctor. This was a situation where at first I thought it was the only answer because I did not know anything else.

I use *Back to Eden* as my major reference as it has been the most complete book I have found. Recently, however, I ran across a book called, *Herbally Yours*, by Penny C. Royal which is an updated version of *Back to Eden* with more current medical information.

Here are a few case histories: My wife began having problems with her monthly cycle. The cramps became very painful and quite a change as she had not experienced this problem when she was just a girl. I developed a compound which eliminated the pain and made it easy for her once again. She is a director of a health spa and one of her employees had this same problem with cramps all her life. When the girl would miss work the first day or so of her cycle, my wife suggested that she take my pills. She did and it helped her. The next month, the day before she was to start, she took a pill and began the next day and wasn't aware of anything which was a bit embarrassing because she was wearing white pants.

Another time, I had taken a doctor friend to see the International Karate Championships at Long Beach. My wife had a sinus headache so I gave her another compound of mine. The doctor asked what it was and where I got it. I told him it was red sage and peppermint and that I made it up myself. He was impressed and asked me to help his wife who was having trouble with swollen paratoid glands. I worked up a compound and it relieved the swelling and pain. He was very happy and offered his medical services for myself and my family at any time for no charge.

I have a long history of a bad back from a football injury dating back to high school days. This was followed after high school by two car accidents just six months apart. I went to a specialist who told me not to lift over twenty five pouunds and no more kenpo for one year and "maybe" it would heal itself. That wasn't good enough for me, so I gradually increased my exercise program. I would, however, have a stiff back and it eventually worked its way into a sciatic nerve pinch. I began working with an herb called nettle and found it would give almost immediate relief, and by the end of the day, I could walk normally again. This went on for three or four years. Once every year I could feel this coming on. I started using the herb, nettle, in conjunction with the linament I developed and eventually healed myself. As soon as I would feel it coming on, I would rub in the linament and begin drinking a tea made from the herb.

An elderly lady at a church I was attending, heard the story and asked what the herb was. I told her and she too relieved her pain caused by a sciatic nerve pinch.

When my middle daughter contracted chicken pox, we took her to the doctor. He told us that calamine lotion was all he could recommend to relieve the itching. I once again looked for an herb to help the situation. I found chickweed. I made about four pints at a time and put it into her bath water. In a matter of a few days, the redness began to go away and the itching stopped. We used the same thing on our youngest daughter and the children of many friends also.

It still amazes me when it works. It has never failed to work either on my immediate family or friends who have asked for help.

Over the years, my family has remained relatively free from illness and very healthy. If ninety percent of illness is psychosomatic, then a positive attitude has helped and in some cases the "bitterness" of my herbs has also helped. In 1977, I started working on putting herbs into capsules and had great success with my compounds eliminating the bitter taste of many herbs. It is much more convenient to take a pill like a vitamin rather than brewing a cup of tea. However, for throat disorders, the tea is most soothing and effective.

When making teas for medicinal purposes, remember these helpful hints:
For leaves and flowers, bring the water to a boil, take it off of the burner and
add the herb, usually one teaspoon per cup. Let it stand for fifteen to twenty
minutes to extract all of the goodness from the herb. Strain and drink the
liquid. I have found that the hot teas taste better, although that is a personal
preference and medicinally, either hot or cold tea would work equally well.

For roots and bark, steep the herb in the water on a low flame, or on low if
you have an electric range, for fifteen to twenty minutes. Again, the purpose is
to extract all of the good from the herb. Strain and drink the liquid.

The best way to start is to first purchase a good book to use for reference.
When you come across an interesting herb such as golden seal, learn all you
can about it and buy it. Golden seal is good for almost everything, a "cure-all"
and a good general tonic. As the need arises, check your book and see what
herbs will cure your cold, flu, etc. If you don't have it, go buy it, and gradually
you will have a pretty good variety. Here are some of the things I have cured
with herbs:

Headaches—Peppermint; one teaspoon per cup of water.
Sinus Headache—Red Sage and Peppermint combined.
Tension—Catnip.
Sciatic Nerve Pinch—Nettle.
Backache—Nettle.
Dandruff—Sage; used as a rinse.
Chicken Pox—Chickweed; used to eliminate redness and itching.
Sore Throat and Tonsilitis—Golden Seal.

These are only a few. For every illness, there is an herb to cure it. Non-
poisonous herbs can not hurt you so when you have any of these or other
problems, treat it as a natural medicine taking three to four cups a day. There
will be no side effects and you will be pleased with the results. Remember, to
use good judgment and moderation in all that you do. Eat a balanced meal
and do some form of exercise, I would recommend Kenpo, but do something.
The use of herbs does not mean eliminating going to a doctor in an emergency. But, by being more aware of your body and keeping it in harmony and
balance, dis-ease and illness will not find a foothold. Learn to be your own
physician and heal yourself.

Here is a list of commonly used herbs:

ANGELICA	MULLEIN
BUCKTHORN	MYRRH
CAMOMILE	NETTLE
CATNIP	FORMOSA OOLONG
CAYENNE	PEPPERMINT
CHICKWEED	PSYLLA
COMFREY	RED CLOVER
CORNSILK	RED RASPBERRY
DANDELION	RED SAGE
FENNEL	SAGE
GINSENG	SARSAPARILLA
GOLDEN ROD	SASSAFRAS
GOLDEN SEAL	SCULLCAP
GOTA KULA	SELF-HEAL
HIMALYAN DARJEERING	SENNA
HYSSOP	SLIPPERY ELM
LOBELIA	VERVAIN
LICORICE	WILD CHERRY
MANDRAKE	YARROW
	YELLOW DOCK

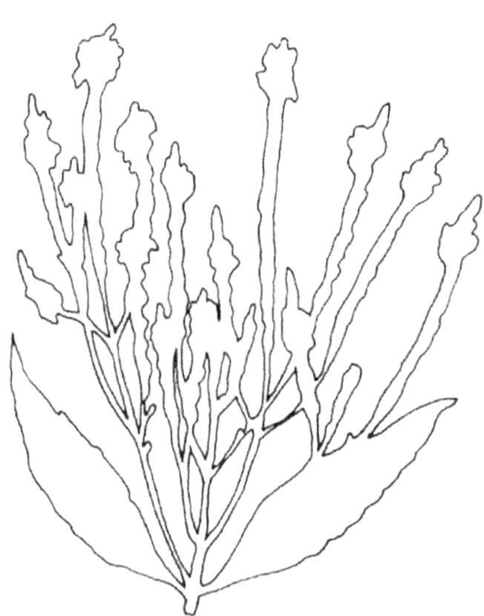

Blue Vervain
Botanical Name: Verbena Hastata

Chamomile
Botanical Name: Anthemis Nobilis

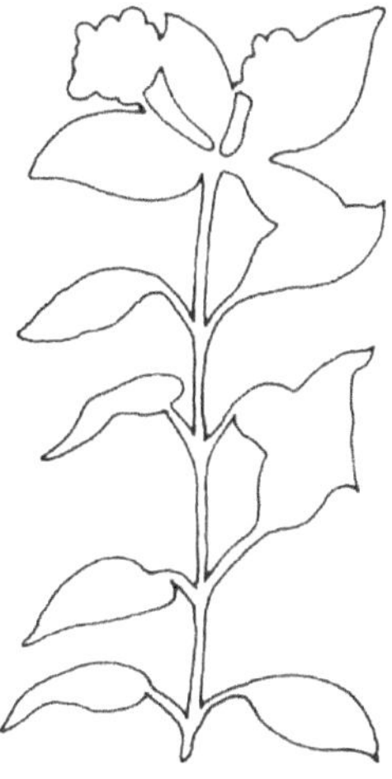

Chickweed
Botanical Name: Stellaria Media

Catnip
Botanical Name: Nepeta Cataria

Dandelion
Botanical Name: Taraxicum Dens-Leonis

Golden Seal
Botanical Name: Hydrastis Canadensis

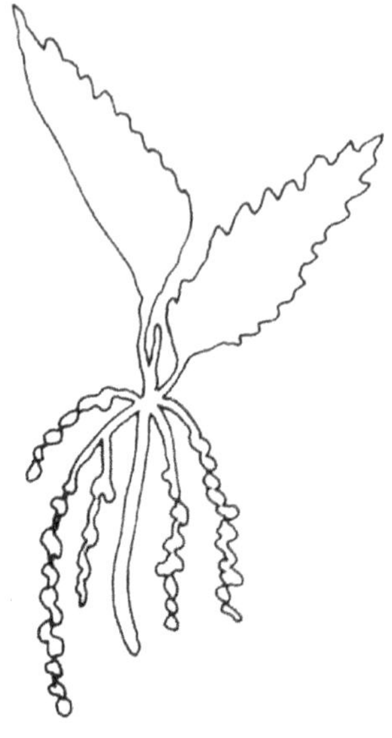

Nettle
Botanical Name: Urtica Dioica

Comfrey
Botanical Name: Symphytum Officinale

Peppermint
Botanical Name: Mentha Piperita

Conclusion

Kenpo has something for everyone. In this book, there are techniques for the beginning student as well as the advanced. Study it well and learn why I believe that Kenpo is the up-coming martial arts experience. It is simplicity in execution and economy in motion with completeness in form.

The student can learn these movements easily and apply the information to practical use. But knowledge is not the ultimate goal. Wisdom is the end, ultimately, and using knowledge is the way to achieve it.

You can gain self-confidence by learning how to protect and defend yourself. You will not find it necessary to prove yourself to anyone. Confidence comes with the ability to handle any situation calmly as they arise. It is my goal to help you develop all aspects of your nature using Kenpo as the scale to balance the mind and body.

ONE-ON-ONE INTERVIEW WITH
MASTER MICHAEL J. PERSONS

By Jose M. Fraguas

How long have you been practicing the martial arts?

"I have been practicing and teaching the martial arts for over 56 years, beginning Feb 6, 1966."

How many styles (Kenpo or other methods) have you trained in?

"I have only trained in one style and that is Kenpo. But under the Kenpo banner, I have studied Original Kenpo/American Kenpo as taught by Grand Master Ed Parker while we were with the (IKKA) International Kenpo Karate Association until 1972. Grand Master Joe Dimmick taught Sam Pai Kenpo/3 Shields Kenpo and I was with him for another thirty years."

Who were your first teachers?

"My first and only teacher was Grand Master Joe Dimmick whom I studied under for 36 years. He began his training with Grand Master Ed Parker in the South Gate School in an old gym Mr. Parker purchased when he returned from his education at BYU. Later Mr. Dimmick moved up to the South Pasadena School which was Mr. Parker's Headquarters."

Would you tell us some interesting stories of your early days in Kenpo?

"Team fighting was always an exciting component of the Internationals. One year it was our Downey school against Grand Master Norris' Tang Soo Do school. They were up six points with one fighter to go in the Brown Belt finals. Brian Sonnenberg stepped up for us and promptly beat his opponent 6-0 and sent it into overtime. We, of course, kept Brian in and they kept their same fighter who had just lost to Brian 6-0. Brian scored another point very quickly and we won the Brown Belt team championship.

I knew Mr. Parker pretty well. At one International's, probably in 1985, I was introducing my wife Kalyani (Ka'uilani), who is Hawaiian and Mr. Parker's wife, Leilani, joined us in the conversation. The wives began to talk, in the usual Hawaiian style."

What Island did you grow up on, and what school did you go to?

"When the conversation got to the question of Kalyani's maiden name, she answered, 'Mossman.' Leilani responded, "We are cousins". Mr. Parker just smiled at me and shrugged his shoulders. Of all the schools and organizations, I picked him, and then I picked my wife, and the circle was complete. At this point, I had known Mr. Parker for 19 years. My wife was probably related to Mr. Parker as well and the Parker and Mossman Ohana/families are related in the Hawaiian culture."

In Kenpo there are sets of self-defense techniques, (per belt), what do these really represent and how important are they?

"The self-defense techniques are an idea of how to get out of any situation you might find yourself in. If someone pushes you or chokes you, what would you do? These self-defense techniques give you an idea of what to do in that situation. I always ask my students, what else could they do in this situation. They have to know the techniques exactly as taught for testing, but they also know it is not the only way. In 7 Winds Kenpo, there are thirty self-defense and freestyle techniques in every level from Orange to 5th Black Belt."

Were you a 'natural' at Kenpo? Did the movements come easily to you?

"I believe that I was a natural. The movements came easy, I think from, previous physical activities: football, basketball, and baseball. I was also exposed to track and soccer in my junior high experience. I started lifting weights when I was 12 and continue to do the Bow Flex in my workout routine today. In 1969 I had a tryout with the California Angels, but I did not make it further than that. I have been blessed with athletic ability that allows me to continue to teach and practice the martial art of Kenpo."

How has your personal expression of Kenpo changed and developed over the years?

"As you age in the martial arts things naturally change. I was fortunate to have grown up in what I call the Golden Era of the martial arts, the '60s and '70s. I saw all of the greatest fighters: Allen Stein, Mike Stone, Chuck Norris, Joe Lewis, and so many others. I also belonged to a great fighting school, Grand Master Dimmick's Downey Kenpo school. We had many State and International champions: Howard Singer, George Hay, and Nat Dominguez. In my early training, it was geared toward tournaments. The largest was Grand Master Ed Parker's annual International Kenpo Karate Championships held in Long Beach, CA. Since the passing of Grand Master Parker, in 1990, the tournament scene just hasn't been the same.

Today I teach with an emphasis on self-defense for the home with weapons that are unfamiliar to traditional Kenpo. I also have a pathway to the 10th Black Degree Belt which entails constant learning and perfecting our technique; even though we know we will never be perfect we still strive for perfection.

What are the most important points in your teaching methods? And what are the most important qualities for a student to become proficient in the Kenpo style?

"One of the most important traits a teacher can have is patience. I may have done Short One a thousand times, but the student is seeing it for the first time, and it can be overwhelming. I like to pose the question of "what if" this or that to anticipate potential scenarios. I encourage that foresight in my students to prepare themselves for the unknown. Always be thinking of different situations wherever you are. The student who will always do the best is the one who is "All In" and one who will practice once or twice a day. Sometimes, this discipline is developed over time and others jump right in from the beginning."

With all the technical changes during the last years, do you think there are still 'pure' styles of Kenpo?

"I know that when we were with Mr. Parker, Mr. Dimmick adhered to his teaching very closely. But every instructor brings something new to the table. Mr. Dimmick had black belts in three different arts; Kenpo, Choy Lai Fut/Hung Gar, and Chito Ryu Karate, so our Kenpo would be slightly different from an instructor who didn't have that experience.

While I only studied with one instructor, I consider myself a good observer and I have over fifty books on martial arts which I have read cover to cover. When I see something that I think will fit into what I am teaching I incorporate it into my art. Possibly the greatest lesson was studying with Mr. Dimmick. He was constantly analyzing his system and making adjustments he felt would improve it. It was in that vein that I conceived 7 Winds Kenpo.

I adopted that creative characteristic inspired by Mr. Dimmick and Mr. Parker and created 27 forms of my own which are part of 7 Winds Kenpo. I have done this in the spirit of Grand Masters Parker and Dimmick of constant change and attempting to improve the art. I believe that Mr. Parker and Mr. Dimmick were constantly changing the art, so I am not sure what pure Kenpo would look like. We went through seven major changes in Sam-Pai Kenpo during my training. I also believe that you can only re-arrange the alphabet so many times and then it is time to perfect your art that is why I created the path to 10th Black in my system, 7 Winds Kenpo.

When I was a white belt, I had 13 self-defense techniques with no names. Later, we progressed to 30 techniques with names, and 52 techniques for brown belt. We were changing all of the time. The structure may be the "pure" aspect of Kenpo; basics, self-defense techniques, and forms."

Do you think different 'styles' are truly important in the art of Kenpo? If so, why?

"I think that style is such a part of Kenpo that I don't believe you can separate it. It is where you began your training and I think every other school would be slightly different to you. I was doing a form one day and another student observed me and said, "You like just like Mr. Dimmick." I thought that was a great compliment. It is also, as I said before, that each instructor will bring something different to the dojo. We had Chinese Kung Fu and Japanese Karate as influences in Mr. Dimmick's teaching due to his training."

What is your opinion of fighting events such as the UFC and Mixed Martial Arts events?

"I think that they are a lot of fun to watch, and they are some of the toughest fighters anywhere. I think the fighters who succeed are the ones with good martial arts training and technique."

Kenpo is nowadays often referred to as a sport... would you agree with this definition or is it a martial art?

"Kenpo was a sport when there were tournaments or at least it had a sports aspect to it. It has always been a martial art with tradition and a spirit and self-defense at its core. Knowing the history and where we fit into the grand scheme of things, I have only taught it as an effective form of self-defense. Mr. Parker used to say that he would teach you 1,000 things and it would be up to you to pick those which suited you best. I like to say that while some bring 100 weapons to a fight, we bring 1,000."

Do you feel that you still have further to go in your studies?

"Yes, absolutely! I have created a pathway for my students to get to 10th Black. It is 30 self-defense techniques, one empty hand form, and 9 weapons forms. We do these from 8th and 9th Black trying to become better at our technique, perfecting it a little more at each level. Once you attain 10th Black you don't stop. You never stop, because you are trying to attain perfection although it will always be just out of reach."

How do you see Kenpo in America at present?

It is hard for me to judge as I am pretty isolated here in South Carolina. I know Grand Master Dimmick and Grand Master Post both teach privately. Master Bob White still has an organization where I believe he puts on a children's tournament annually. Other instructors I have known are no longer teaching. I am sure studios or dojos are operating but I don't have any contact with them. As a method of self-defense, I believe that there is none better than Kenpo, so then, all you have to do is find an instructor."

Do you think it helps the Kenpo student physically to train with weapons?

"I do believe it helps Kenpo students physically to train with weapons. I have at least one weapon on every level from Orange to 5th Black. Mr. Parker use to say that a weapon is just an extension of your arm. I have adapted many traditional weapons by applying Kenpo techniques. My students love this aspect of their training and many of the weapons are interchangeable because of the principles applied in each form. They are taught so that they can be substituted with everyday weapons. A broom or rake can become a staff, a knife from your utensils drawer can become a weapon and even a hammer can become a Tonfa or a club -- *weapons of opportunity.*"

How do the Kenpo styles differ from other martial arts methods when applying the techniques in a self-defense situation?

"I think that Kenpo might be the most structured in that we have basics, forms, and self-defense techniques in every level up to 1st Black. Virtually every Kenpo Dojo has training booklets or a pre-set list of things the student must do to promote to the next level. In the Black Belt levels, there are no more basics as the student has had them all by the time they reach Black Belt. I have been in some schools where you just go off by yourself and practice techniques given by the instructor. I think the best way to learn is to have a structure. The student can also judge their progress and as all of the techniques in a given level become more familiar the student is aware that it will soon be time to test."

When teaching the art of Kenpo, what is the most important element -- self-defense or sport?

"Self-defense has always been the priority. The sports aspect was kind of a reward for all of the hard practice. Also, there are many things you can do in a self-defense situation but cannot do in a tournament. Even today there are rules to every form of competition but on the street, anything goes. The consistent training in the self-defense aspect is what leads to becoming a real martial artist and making it a part of your life."

Forms and sparing, what's the proper ratio in training?

"While they are both parts of the whole training, they are also separate. When you are young you don't like forms much and like to spar. Today we don't physically spar that much, but it is a part of our training. We have freestyle techniques and even forms called Fighting Warrior Sets 1-8, Orange through 1st Black. The self-defense techniques help you in a situation where there is a committed attack, and the freestyle techniques give you an idea of what to do in a combat situation. It is the art of fighting without fighting, as Bruce Lee once said. We prepare for any situation and hope that it never comes, but if it should, we will be ready for almost anything."

Do you have any general advice that you would care to pass on to the practitioners in general?

"Find a great instructor and stick with him. Make sure you have similar beliefs, and that you can trust him. Then be "All In" and practice, practice, practice. The rewards for this are beyond explanation. When the student begins, they are usually clumsy and can't quite get the moves down, then as an instructor, you see the lights come on one day and they have the moves down pat. Time begins to pass quicker and quicker and soon they have reached the black belt level. It seems the farther you go the farther you want to go. The white belt levels: orange, purple, blue, and green are like high school. The three brown belt levels are college and the black belt levels are your graduate work where you begin to understand what it means to be a martial artist."

What do you consider to be the major changes in the art since you began training?

"I don't believe that you have the large organizations of the '60s and '70s. While there are many schools out there, I believe they are not part of an organization for the most part, except for Tae Kwon Do and other Korean arts. I also don't think there is so much formality. We work out in our GI bottoms and a tee shirt, but for testing, I require a full uniform. Of course, it is also 56 years later, and I have no desire to have a commercial school. Teaching privately, one on one, you get to teach who you want to teach and with that, I keep a balance of tradition and a less formal atmosphere."

Who would you like to have trained with that you have not (dead or alive)?

"Masutatsu Oyama. He was the first martial artist I can remember taking notice of and anyone who killed 56 bulls with his bare hands, had to have something special going on. Mas Oyama was Korean and migrated to Japan where he began to teach Chinese Kempo, (the Asian spelling of Kenpo). I have tried running through the snow barefooted and with only GI bottoms on, although I never stood under a waterfall in the snow of a cold winter day as he did. But he did inspire me to begin my training in our Downey School."

What would you say to someone interested in starting to learn Kenpo?

"I would tell them that they have picked the right art, and now find a good Kenpo instructor to train under. I have observed martial arts for 56 years and when I look at other styles, I find Kenpo is contained in those same elements that make up the other styles.

Speak with the instructor and see what they teach and if it follows some structure with basics, katas, and self-defense techniques. I like structure and I believe it is the way you can tell if you are making progress.

If it is a commercial school observe a class if you can. See how the class is conducted and how the students respond. If they are respectful, then you can assume that the instructor is teaching that in class. If they are punks, well, you may want to keep looking."

What is it that keeps you motivated after all these years?

"The desire to perfect my art keeps me motivated. My students also keep me motivated. If you have great students, it is a joy to teach them and watch them progress. Just like your children, you want your students to surpass your accomplishments. There is also confidence in continuing to train that you can take care of yourself and your family, should the need arise."

What is/was your philosophical basis for your Kenpo training?

"I grew up in a Christian home and when I was 17, I stopped going to church and wanted to find the "truth." I studied all the major religions of the world and all of the various Christian churches. I studied the occult and two secret brotherhoods.

All of the time I was searching, I would bounce what I was reading or being told against what the Bible teaches. Then one day I was listening to a favorite Bible teacher of mine, and he was doing a study on the mathematical probability of Jesus being who he said he was. The presentation was so convincing that at the end of it the teacher says, you now have a decision to make. Jesus was either a good man, crazy or the Son of God. And if you believe he is the Son of God, then what are you going to do about it?

The truth was with me all of the time. In my search for the "truth," I only found someone else's truth and not the "truth". I am fortunate that all my students are Christians."

Do you have a particularly memorable Kenpo experience that has remained an inspiration for your training?

"One day I was sparring with a former teacher of mine, we were both black belts at the time. Nat Dominguez was a State Champ and International Champ as well. He was fast like Sugar Ray Leonard. He attacked and I was blocking everything he was throwing, and the final punch was headed for my face, and I caught it in my left hand. We were both shocked and Mr. Dimmick just happened to enter at that very moment, and he cautioned us, that we were getting to know each other's techniques too well.

One last memory, I was standing watching a weapons competition at the Internationals when Mr. Parker joined me. The next contestant was a woman who looked a little dis-shoveled with no GI that could be recognized. Her form used butter knives. She just moved them around like she was stirring chocolate milk, obviously not a martial artist but she paid her entry fee, so she got to perform. Mr. Parker said to me. "Who let her in?" I responded, "you did, it is your tournament." He laughed and walked away shaking his head."

After all these years of training and experience, could you explain the meaning of the practice of Kenpo?

"I look at life as self-defense; physically, mentally, and spiritually. Kenpo is the physical aspect of that triangle. Be ready for whatever might come your way. The conditioning is also an aspect of the physical part of the triangle. This then sets up the mental which is educating yourself on various subjects so that when you are confronted with different ideas you can "defend" yourself. Also, going through the manuals and learning all that is being taught, is the beginning of learning and teaches you how to learn.

My student, Dr. Ken Horup once told me that this taught him how to study and he is a doctor. The Chinese martial artists taught the 5 Graces; History, Government, Art, Healing, and self-defense to balance every aspect of the student's character.

I love history and study it constantly, and also enjoy researching our Ancestry. It helps to clarify where these ancestors came from and better insight as to who they were.

It is good to be well versed in government, especially, today with all of the bickering and fighting about who is right. Again, know what you believe and why you believe it.

I am an author of three books and the fourth soon to be released, which is the first in a trilogy. I have written 17 training manuals for 7 Winds Kenpo, yet to be published. I have dabbled in drawing so there is that also on the artistic side of things.

I have been an herbalist since Jan 1972 and have also written a book on the subject that I will someday publish. I worked in a Chiropractic office for ten years and learned that aspect of healing also.

Fifty-sex years of martial arts and I believe I have the 5 Graces covered."

How do you think a practitioner can increase his or her under-standing of the spiritual aspect of the art?

"Most schools don't teach anything spiritual because there are too many different beliefs. If you were sitting outside the Shaolin Monastery you would have a Buddhist frame of reference. Because we are all Christian in my school, there is a lot of discussion on our beliefs. As we progress both spiritually and physically, I call it sanctification.

When you are a new Christian, you want to believe but you don't have all of the tools of a Christian of twenty years or more. So, gradually as you grow you are better able to give a reason for what you believe. It is the same physically. When you first begin you learn Short Form 1 and it is difficult until you finally get it. Later you are doing complex forms as well as weapon sets. Then as you look back on your beginnings in martial arts you can see just how far you have come and how much confidence you now have."

Is there anything lacking in the way martial arts is taught today compared to how they were in your beginnings?

"Some of the old drills, perhaps, in my beginnings we did something called 4 across. Because there might be 20-40 students in the class we had to line up and take our turn performing blocks, kicks, punches, etc. Then you would match up with a partner, still in 4 across, and one of you would punch and the other would block. This toughened our forearms and our legs, and it was difficult and painful. I am not sure students today would "put up with that". I still do this in my classes even though there is only a single student in a class. If you have a structure, I believe it lessens the possibility of "lack" in your training. You are trying to cover all aspects and you have a plan to follow.

We were there for self-defense purposes and wanted to learn how to fight. Students today come to you for all kinds of reasons from self-defense to an exercise class. The training was just tougher back in the day."

Could I ask you what you consider to be the most important qualities of a successful Kenpo practitioner?

"Dedication: Striving every day to be a little better than you were the day before. And consistently striving every day to do something martial arts related, even if it is thinking about a few of the "what ifs" scenarios. My number one student, Dr. Ken Horup, practiced twice a day for years and I believe that today he practices at least once a day. He is a 9th Degree Black Belt progressing towards his 10th.

My other Black Belt, Vince Mucci, a 6th Degree Black Belt, has the same dedication and practices at least 5-6 times a week. Both of these men are "All In" in Kenpo and their Christian lives as well."

What advice would you give to students on the question of supplementary training (running, weights, et cetera)?

"I think that all of these exercises are great and should be exploited to the best of the student's capabilities. I walk, ride bikes, do Bow Flex, and stretch trying to do all that I can to stay in condition. I also do the Masters-level Kenpo training.

It consists of an empty hand form, 9 weapons sets, and 30 self-defense techniques. The first 15 are takeaways; guns, knives, and clubs, and the last 15 are freestyle techniques. I feel this is a well-rounded training routine. Again, we are working toward the perfection of our technique and art both with weapons and the empty hand."

What do you see as the most important attributes of a student?

"I think a good character is most important. I don't want to teach someone who is going to go right out and hurt someone. Fighting should be a last resort.

Dedication would be a close second and, of course, you can't always determine this from an initial interview. But time will tell and most students who are not there for the correct reasons won't last. I guess that is why the Shaolin Temple used to train you in horse stances for up to 2 years before showing you anything else. No one today would put up with that, but it was a way of weeding out the bad pupils."

Why is it, in your opinion, that a lot of students start falling away after two-three years of training?

"Sometimes it doesn't take that long. When I was a White Belt, Mr. Dimmick said in class one day, "Look around at the 40 students in this class, because most of them won't make it to the first level. Sure enough, there were only about 15-20 in the Orange Belt class, and it gradually shrunk at every level.

I think some people don't realize what they are getting themselves into. In my initial interview with Mr. Dimmick, I told him that I wouldn't stop until I got my Black Belt. His response was, "Sure. Do you know how many times I hear that?" I said but I mean it.

I was about his 3rd or 4th wave of Black Belts, but 36 years later I was his number one along with Andre Ouellette. We both received our 10th Degree Black on the same day."

Have there been times when you felt fear in your training?

"No! As I stated before, we had a lot of great fighters in our Downey School but none of them were bullies or deliberately trying to hurt you. We fought hard, but that is what made us better. I have to say that in 12 years at the Internationals and other tournaments I never ran into anyone who was out to hurt me nor caused me to fear them."

What are your thoughts on the future of the arts?

"The future of the arts is in our hands as instructors, but unfortunately, systems die out for lack of someone to step up and carry on the traditions of the school. Kenpo is a good example of that when Mr. Parker passed in December 1990, he did not have someone to carry on for him and as a consequence, many tried on their own to step up but to no avail.

I have taken steps to preserve my art, 7 Winds Kenpo. I have 17 training manuals from Orange Belt to 10th Degree Black Belt; I hope to publish them one day. For each level of training, the students receive a training manual. As Dr. Horup is going for his 10th Degree Black Belt he has all of the manuals. Vince Mucci is going for his 7th Degree Black Belt and has manuals up to his level. Emily Buck is going for 3rd Brown Belt and Tristan Horup is going for Green Belt and each has its own manual. This way they will always have a reference point to go back to and check if they are doing things correctly.

The only thing better would be to have a step-by-step book with pictures so that the student could see the moves rather than interpret them from the manuals. If they continue to train, it wouldn't be that hard but if they had a period of time off, it might be harder to come back to the training.

In these manuals, I have described every move: block, kick, punch, and stance. I have cataloged every technique and form so no one can claim that they trained with me, and this is how I used to do it. Outside of the written word, we are going to start doing videos of the various forms and techniques to keep for posterity.

The novels I have written -- *The 7 Secret Scrolls* and *The Warriors of Chilandra,* which is Book One in the *"Beyond Shazandras"* Series, are in the martial arts adventure genre. They have 7 Winds Kenpo authentic techniques described in the fight scenes. My goal is that if someone picks up any of my novels 100 years from now, they will be inspired by Kenpo to begin their own wonderful journey as I have. When the instruction manuals are in print, and the videos can be accessed it will keep 7 Winds Kenpo alive forever."

NOTES